Truth Is Reason

Faith of a Scientist

John W Jensen

© 2020 John W Jensen

All Rights Reserved

Cover by Daniel Jensen

*To Stacey and the kids,
my reason for everything*

and

*To Ryan Olsen
who challenged me
to write a one-page essay on faith.
Unfortunately,
I was unable to stay on topic
and have shown a rather
embarrassing disregard
for the page limit.*

Table of Contents

Preface .... *vii*

God *1*

   Knowing God Exists 3

   Spiritual Experience 11

   Faith in God 21

   A Child of God 31

   We Lived in Heaven 39

   A Simulation 49

   Perspective... 57

   I've a Mother There 67

Christ *79*

   An Atonement... 81

   The Savior.. 91

   Sin's Consequence 97

   Hope Born of Repentance................................. 103

   Where Is Heaven? 111

   Saving Ordinances 125

   Authorized Religion.. 137

Holy Ghost..*145*
    Spiritual Communication..147
    Unanswered Questions..159
    Knowing the Church is True 167
    We Thank Thee, O God, For a Prophet..............179
    Baptism of Fire...193
Conclusion *205*

Preface

Shortly after I began my PhD in physics, I got into a religious discussion with a visiting professor. He had a question about one of my beliefs, and I gave him a simple answer. I wanted to provide him with more information, so I later decided to use this relatively new thing called Google. I wasn't quite prepared for the volume of troubling information the internet spat back at me.

As a PhD student with a carefully cultivated ego, I decided I should be smart enough to sit down and formulate a general, rationally-based, metaphysical theory of the restored gospel of Jesus Christ. It didn't take too much dipping into difficult topics before my ego was completely crushed, and my testimony was shaken.

About that time, I was asked to be the ward mission leader, which meant I taught the most basic gospel principles to new members of the church. I was grateful to leave the difficult topics behind and teach the stuff I knew backwards and forwards.

But something had changed. I thought I could quarantine all my questions and doubts to the difficult parts of the gospel, but life found a way to slosh and spill these doubts everywhere. I could still recite the basic definition of faith or repentance as I taught the class, but I wasn't sure what I knew about faith or repentance anymore.

The scriptures say Christ is the foundation on which we must build,[1] but how was I supposed to go about that? I honestly thought that was exactly what I had done before everything all of a sudden became so shaky.

Some people might call this a full-blown crisis of faith. It certainly felt like a crisis. No matter how hard I tried, I just couldn't see how the simple, primary-class understanding of the gospel would ever cover the spiritual complexity I discovered as an adult.

What I wish I would have understood during that time is this process is completely normal. We must all traverse this difficult, but wonderous, path from youthful faith and simple understanding toward a deep and expansive testimony of Jesus Christ.

A successful spiritual maturation process includes three steps: a person discovers spiritual complexity, they explore the complexity, and they fold that complexity

---

[1] Hel. 5:12

back into the simple gospel basics they were taught before.

As a bishop, I counsel young adults and others going through this, often painful, spiritual maturation process. I find that they work through steps one and two fairly quickly but often struggle with step three. This usually results in reduced participation in the church or the gospel—most often both.

This spiritual maturation process has been going on since the beginning of time. The major difference in the Information Age is that the internet helps people discover spiritual complexity at a far earlier age than in the past. The internet also helps people explore spiritual complexity at a break-neck pace. The problem seems to be that many people gain a deep, expert understanding of spiritual complexity without spending a similar effort gaining a deep, expert understanding of gospel basics. When they try to move on to step three, they just can't see how this multifaceted, complex topic is ever going to merge back with the ordinary, simple topics they learned before. In reality, the simple topics of the gospel are far richer than we realize.

We see this type of problem in the young man who can practically recite each version of the First Vision but does not understand faith well enough to see why he has to believe any of it without proof. Or the woman who leaves the church because of an atheistic argument but doesn't understand the nature of God well enough to see that particular argument doesn't even apply to Latter-day Saint theology.

I had the same problem during my google-induced crisis. I quickly researched every controversial religious topic online but didn't know how everything fit back into gospel basics. It was only after I began applying the same enthusiasm to the lessons for my gospel principle class that I began to see my understanding was shallow. A shallow understanding of a foundational principle cannot support complexity for long.

We see this in completely secular situations as well. Why did I get a bad grade in calculus? It wasn't because I didn't understand calculus; it was because my understanding of algebra was shallow. Why, during my driver's education class, did I jump the curb and almost hit that one house? I thought I knew the exact function of the pesky third pedal called the clutch, but apparently that understanding was shallow.

In a similar manner, when discussing the Church of Jesus Christ of Latter-day Saints, commonly known as the Mormon Church or LDS Church, and its relationship to mainstream Christianity, the default question has always been, "Are Mormons Christian?" This question cannot be answered if the person only has a shallow understanding of Latter-day Saint theology.

A similar question is, "Are bananas berries?" Using the fundamental biological definition of berries, the answer is yes; bananas are berries. Most of us are not familiar with the biological definition of berries though, so when we ask about berries, we mean something quite different than a banana.

When the average person asks, "Are Mormons Christians?" if you were to say, "no", they would think you don't believe Jesus Christ is your savior. If you were to say, "yes", they would think the restored gospel of Jesus Christ is just another flavor, among hundreds, within mainstream Christianity. Both answers are incorrect. This question cannot be answered without first gaining a deeper understanding of the restored gospel of Jesus Christ.

This is the objective of this book: to deepen a person's understanding of the gospel using a rational, almost scientific approach. Don't we get into trouble when we apply logic and reason to the gospel, you might ask? Yes, sometimes we get into trouble, but it isn't because the gospel is not reasonable or logical. We humans are just good at convincing ourselves we are more logical than we actually are. On the other hand, we all know testimony cannot be built by logic and reason alone, but we sometimes forget that testimony is fragile or misplaced if logic and reason are completely ignored.

My primary audience is the rationally-minded thinker, but I specifically stay away from academic jargon and use a down-to-earth, conversational style with many practical examples. I do not attempt to discuss scientific evidence for religion or get bogged down discussing complex scientific theories and their effect on religious thought.

My secondary audience is the Latter-day Saint who is struggling, but I purposefully do not discuss controversial topics so as to not distract from the deep exploration of gospel basics. Because of this, I do not provide a complete theology in this book. What I do provide are the waypoints we must all traverse on our spiritual journey. For example, a Latter-day Saint must, at some point, contemplate the existence of God and personal revelation. In a similar way, a scientist studying light must explore reflection and diffraction.

I discuss the most common waypoints, but the path you take in your spiritual journey will be unique. And so it must be *your* path. The difficult parts of the spiritual journey are ultimately yours to navigate. Everyone reacts to spiritual complexity differently, and everyone folds complexity into their life differently. What doesn't change is the foundation on which we are to build.

The simple foundation in Christ we gained as we first learned about the gospel is not sufficient for the mansion he intends for us. That foundation must be deepened and expanded as we mature spiritually. This process is guaranteed to shake the structure of our current testimony at times. Still, as we learn to trust in the Lord, not only do we strengthen our foundation, we begin to build a relationship with him—which has always been, and ever will be, the true aim.

PART ONE

God

God

Chapter 1

Knowing God Exists

"I got a stool and looked in Dad's top drawer," Tom stammered while wringing his hands.

"What's wrong?" I asked. "What did you find?" I wasn't sure what could be so scary in a sock and underwear drawer.

"Dad is the Easter Bunny!" Tom blurted. He hesitated and then struggled to maintain some semblance of hope. "There still might be an Easter Bunny for other kids, but Dad is the Easter Bunny for us."

It was just a few days after Easter, and my six-year-old brother, Tom, had discovered a secret. My dad always kept a little Easter candy for his personal stash before hiding the rest for the kids—a practice I faithfully keep to this day. When Tom found the contraband goods with the original packaging from each type of candy found on Easter morning, he put two and two together and discovered the truth.

Atheists and agnostics use experiences such as this to argue that belief in God is as childish as the Easter Bunny, Santa Claus, or any other number of childhood fantasies across cultures. What most people don't recognize is these experiences can be used to argue *for* the existence of God just as powerfully.

Anyone who has undergone a similar childhood experience can understand how it can be used to argue for the existence of God by noticing that Tom didn't say, "I found out the Easter Bunny doesn't exist." He said, "Dad is the Easter Bunny." Tom didn't question the existence of the Easter Bunny, because his existence was simple fact. Every Easter, the thing called "Easter Bunny" left candy for him. What Tom found out that day was that his understanding of the thing called "Easter Bunny" was quite wrong. Of course, the "bunny" part of the label hadn't helped much.

As a child, I wanted to be a scientist when I grew up. I thought scientists spent all day in white lab coats playing with cool, physics-based toys, only interrupted by the occasional explosion to make things exciting. Now that I am a scientist, with a PhD in physics, I know the truth. I spend all day in front of a computer and have never once worn a white lab coat. This doesn't mean scientists don't exist; it just means my understanding of scientists as a child was quite wrong.

Most arguments for and against the existence of God don't actually argue for or against the existence of God. They argue for or against a particular attribute we commonly ascribe to God.

Spending lots of time arguing about God's omnipotence, for example, is discussing omnipotence not existence. There is primarily one argument that specifically talks about God's existence. In fact, it is the only necessary argument on the topic of God in any form.

This argument goes something like this: If God were to exist, he would have significantly more power and ability than us, and he would be free to use that power or ability as he sees fit. Therefore, God could choose to perfectly hide himself from us or perfectly make himself known to us. Thus, if we want to personally find out if God exists, we must approach him on his terms, not ours.

To understand the strength of this argument, let's look at naked mole rats:

Naked mole rats are small creatures, relatively weak by themselves, and because they live their lives almost entirely underground, they are mostly blind. Naked mole rats still have features that are charming in their own way. Their underground tunnel networks are impressive. Their eusocial behaviors are of interest, and their incredible longevity and innate resistance to cancer have attracted the interest of scientists all over the world.

It is fair to say humans have significantly more power and ability than naked mole rats. We may not have god-like powers when compared to them, but the relationship is close enough to god-like for our purposes.

Let's say you travel to one of the many naked mole rat laboratories around the globe where cancer scientists have whole colonies living in networks of plastic tubes. You could sit and watch each individual go about its life as part of the colony. You could monitor the queen busily producing and nursing new members of the colony, or you could monitor the lowest member of the colony who spends each day searching for food.

None of the naked mole rats would be aware of your presence—they are mostly blind. You would be free to never interfere in any of their lives or to drastically interfere in all of their lives. For example, it would be entirely within your power to remove an individual from the colony and conduct a special test or give a special reward. Which particular individual you removed would be completely up to you. You could choose one at random, or you could have a specific set of conditions that must be met by the individual.

As a human, you exist regardless of whether you constantly interfere in the colony or never interfere in the colony. You would still exist no matter how much the mole rats sit and argue about your existence. The appropriate question for the naked mole rat is not, "Do humans exist?" but, "If humans were to exist, how would I find out about it?"

In a similar way, the first and most fundamental question on the topic of God is not, "Does God exist?" but, "If God were to exist, how would I find out about it?" This is the question which the only necessary argument on God answers. It can be used by both the theist and atheist. The part they tend to disagree on is *how* to find out about the existence of God.

Notice we haven't yet talked about any commonly proposed characteristics of God, such as omnipotence or benevolence. God only needs significantly more power than humans, along with free will. With these two characteristics, God could choose to always perfectly hide himself from humans. If he did this, he would exist, but no one would know about it, nor could anyone ever know about it. We see a form of this scenario as a common trope in science fiction when aliens have cloaking devices or other such technology.

In our example, no matter how much naked mole rats scurry in their plastic tubes, no matter how much they dig or smell or feel, they could never find a human unless you wanted them to find you. Likewise, no matter how much a human searches, no matter how much they probe or test or explore or reason, they could never find God unless God wanted them to find him. That is what it means to be significantly more powerful than us.

Therefore, right from the beginning, the only necessary argument on God absolutely excludes the strict atheist position that God doesn't exist. As we discuss more characteristics of God in later chapters, atheists may feel like they get a foot in the door again, but at this most fundamental level, no one can categorically say God doesn't exist, only that he hasn't made himself known to them yet.

This only necessary argument on God is not often discussed in the open market of religious thought because of its strong Latter-day Saint flavor, which comes through in the conclusion of the argument. If we would like to know if God exists, we must approach him on his terms, not ours. Reading scripture helps. Talking to church leaders helps. Thinking about God logically helps. But when all is said and done, we must approach him directly—on his terms. We must get on our knees and begin a relationship with him.

Approaching God directly has been the kernel of the restored gospel of Jesus Christ from the moment Joseph Smith first stepped foot in the Sacred Grove seeking answers from God, to the moment the missionary, Sunday school teacher, or parent asked you to do the same.

Yes, our personal understanding of God before approaching him may be as far off as Tom's understanding of the Easter Bunny, but we set aside our preconceived notions and approach him nonetheless. The very core of the restored gospel is this: anyone can speak to God, and we believe God cares enough to listen and answer.

Chapter 2

Spiritual Experience

My youngest daughter, Ruth, is just learning how to talk. Her vocabulary amounts to, "Da Da," "Ma Ma," and "Dágum." We're not quite sure what the last one means yet.

Like most kids her age, she loves cell phones. She often puts the phone to her cheek and uses all of her three vocabulary words.

When my wife, Stacey, calls my work phone, Ruth sometimes loudly demands to speak to me. Stacey gives the phone to her, and I say something like, "How are you doing today?" or, "Are you helping Mommy?" I'm often met by nothing but breathing on the other line. I don't even get one of her three words. The silence is only broken by the periodic beep when her cheek touches a button. Sometimes she even hangs up on me, though usually by accident.

I often wonder what is going through her developing brain. Does she recognize that she is actually talking to her father? Does she have any concept of me being absent, yet still present? Does she think the phone is just some toy with a recording of my voice?

If we just look at the facts, Ruth is horrible at telephone communication. She doesn't know how to operate the device, and very little actual communication takes place. If I were to act logically or rationally, I wouldn't allow her to use a phone until she understands what it is and how to use it. But if I did this, I would miss my favorite stage, coming up in a year or so, where she learns how to grab the phone and say, "Hi Daddy!" with the purest delight in her voice—even if all my questions thereafter get just a yes, no, or more breathing.

Luckily, Ruth doesn't wait to use phones until she understands everything about them. She is willing to learn by experience.

We all tend to learn by experience in this life. It helps to pick up as many facts as we can along the way, but there are just too many facts in life for anyone to get more than a smattering before even the longest of short lives is abruptly ended.

It should be no surprise that we learn about God by spiritual experiences. In fact, spiritual experience is the foundation for faith in God. Why is this the case? If God were to exist, why would he choose spiritual experience and not some other foundation? The answer is clear once we understand exactly why life is lived by experience in the first place.

To illustrate this, let's assume you befriend a woman who is absolutely color-blind from birth. Not only can she not see red and green, but she can't see any color at all. Everything is black and white to her. She has lived a relatively normal life, and only has to make minor adjustments to account for her complete color blindness. Ironically, she is a physicist with specialties in electromagnetism, so she knows all the mathematical equations that describe light. She knows exactly the frequencies of light that correspond to each visible color. She even took a class on biophysics and understands perfectly the function of the light-sensing cones and rods in the human eye. And just out of curiosity, she did research where she watched brain scans of people who were looking at colored objects, and she knows the retinue of emotions that colors induce in a person's brain. One might say she has a perfect knowledge of the facts behind color. She has just never experienced color.

One day, you are eating dinner together at a restaurant down on the beach. Palm trees sway in the breeze. A luscious park and public gardens stand just a few feet away. An expansive sunset fills the sky with purples and pinks. Sparse clouds break into a rainbow over the brilliant mountains. The vivid scene burns itself into your memory permanently.

Your new friend glances up from her meal, makes some offhand comment about how the frequencies in the sunset probably range from the mid-seven-hundred nanometers all the way to five-eighty nanometers or so. She then turns back to her meal and continues to eat, relatively unaffected by the scene.

In a strange turn of events, the palm tree directly above your friend drops a coconut which crashes into the back of her head. She blacks out for a brief moment, and as her vision returns, she miraculously can see all color. After blinking a few times and gingerly touching the back of her head, she glances up at the scene. Colors soak into her vision, pushing tears to her eyes. Her mouth opens, but she cannot speak. As she lowers her gaze to the table, even the relatively drab few colors represented in her meal overwhelm her emotions.

The question is, did she gain any new knowledge by experiencing color? She already knew the math and the neurological effects of sensing color, but did she understand anything new after experiencing it firsthand?

A form of this argument was first proposed by the philosopher Frank Jackson in 1982.[1] Most people tend to think the woman has learned something new upon seeing color for the first time, but there is an argument that if the woman had an absolutely *perfect* understanding of everything to do with color, she would not learn anything new.

I don't intend to take sides in this argument. Either position is compatible with what I will now discuss relating to spiritual experience.

In the example of the color-blind woman, we see there are two types of knowledge, factual knowledge and experiential knowledge. If you argue the color-blind woman gained new knowledge on seeing color for the first time, you would say the two types of knowledge are distinct; there is something about experience that an eternity of facts cannot teach. If you argue she did not learn anything new, you would say everything is factual knowledge, but you would also have to admit that experiential knowledge still exists as a sort of practical shortcut. A person can get the gist of something through experience without understanding the facts behind it.

---

[1] Jackson, Frank. "Epiphenomenal Qualia." *The Philosophical Quarterly*, Vol. 32, No. 127. (Apr., 1982), pp. 127-136.

We see these two types of knowledge in play all the time. A person with an advanced degree starts a new job, but he must be trained by the person with only a high school diploma . . . and thirty years' experience. A young couple read multiple books on how to be good parents but then call their aged parents at midnight, lamenting over the fact their two-year-old isn't acting the way the books say he should act. A young lady expecting her first child takes an all-inclusive, six-week course on labor and delivery that comes with a thick book, but in the middle of hard labor throws the book across the delivery room and demands that her husband stomp on it.

Factual knowledge is easily captured in books, classes, and lectures. Experiential knowledge is hardly captured at all by anyone but the person experiencing it. For this reason, factual knowledge lends itself well to science, technology, math, and a number of other fields our modern society values highly. Experiential knowledge is represented more in the arts than the sciences. It is subjective, hard to explain to others, sometimes hard to explain to ourselves, and often takes years to scarcely begin to learn. In our modern society of instant communication, constant entertainment, quick travel, and incredible technological and scientific advancement, it's no wonder factual knowledge is praised by everyone while experiential knowledge is an afterthought or taken for granted.

Spiritual experience, as the label might suggest, relies almost entirely on experiential knowledge. The woman who prays to God for the first time and feels what she believes is God touching her heart has *a* spiritual experience. A woman who prays to God consistently over the years and begins to recognize the often subtle communication between God and his child, that woman *has* spiritual experience. She is becoming spiritually experienced, or experienced in spiritual things.

If God were to exist, why would he rely on experiential knowledge? Because factual knowledge works best with simple concepts, like math or science. The building blocks of facts must be stacked from the bottom up. Factual knowledge cannot explain complex things unless you start with a foundation of simple facts. Experiential knowledge doesn't require the same basis in simple fact, and therefore, it can grant understanding of complex topics without going into complex detail.

If I were to travel to a third-world country and find someone who has never used a computer, what is the best way to teach him to use one? Pure factual knowledge would start with a class on electronics and solid-state physics. Experiential knowledge would just hand the person a computing device, maybe give them a few pointers, and then let them experiment.

Learning by experience, whether in life or spirituality, can be a messy proposition, filled with more errors than successes, but learning by experience allows us to move forward without needing to understand every step of the way first. We can fall in love without taking courses in sociology and psychology first. We can have a child without getting a degree in reproductive physiology and neonatal childhood development. We can be a parent without first getting extensive training in childhood education, nutrition, pediatric medicine, culinary arts, financial administration, counseling, risk communication, circadian sleep cycles, and biohazard material removal.

Can you imagine what it would be like to learn of spiritual things using only factual knowledge? We would need to understand exactly how prayers get sent to God before we would ever pray. We would need to understand how God's mind processes millions of prayers at a time before knowing our prayer was heard. When God answered our prayer, we would need to know every lever he pulled and every button he pushed, before believing the answer came from him and not coincidence.

The simple truth is that none of us know the facts behind how God works. Because of this, we have only a few options left to us. We can refuse to pray because we don't know how prayer actually lets us talk to God. We can wait to pray until we convince ourselves prayer works by subjecting it to rigorous scientific studies. Or, like my daughter Ruth and her phone, we can pray to our Father when we barely know what prayer is, even if our meager efforts at communication start out with little more than, "Hi, Daddy!" followed by lots of silence.

We don't need to understand everything about God before we approach him, just like we don't need to understand everything about life before we start living it.

This is the beginning of faith.

Chapter 3

Faith in God

At about the age of nine or ten, I lost my brand-new watch in a field of weeds behind my childhood home. This wasn't just any watch; I had saved my money for weeks to purchase it. As my brothers abandoned the search to go play some other game, I sat in the weeds, pushing back at discouragement while the size of the weed patch began to sink in.

I finally decided to pray to find my watch.

I had been taught to pray to God when I needed help. I had even heard multiple stories from family members praying to find lost items, so deciding to pray was a natural choice. To my young mind, all I needed was faith, and my prayer would be answered.

I said a short prayer and got up to look again. With my simple faith I assumed I would immediately find it, or at least after no more than ten minutes of searching. When that ten minutes came and went with no watch, I figured something must be wrong. Maybe God didn't like that I was sitting when I prayed. I tried a kneeling prayer, followed by another ten minutes of looking. Maybe God didn't like that I was saying a silent prayer. I tried a vocal prayer, followed by ten more minutes of nothing.

After three or four different varieties of prayer, with three or four different episodes of searching, I still found nothing. I had no idea what I was doing wrong. All the stories about prayer and faith made it sound so easy. I finally gave up and decided to just find it myself.

I divided the field of weeds into sections in my mind and commenced to search every last bit of that blasted field. After a good two or three hours, I had searched from front to back, sided to side, and everything in between with no results. It was getting dark, and my mother had called me in for dinner at least twice.

I finally despaired. I decided to say one last prayer, which, in my youthful fervor, went something like this, "Heavenly Father, I really, really, really want my watch . . . but if you just don't want me to have it, I guess I'll try my best to be OK with that."

I got up from my prayer and decided to take three more steps worth of searching. The first and second steps yielded much of the same, nothing but weeds. On the third, I stepped on my watch.

At first, this experience seems to simply reinforce the basic idea of praying in faith to receive some blessing, with the added lesson that it may take a long time or a lot of effort before you receive your blessing. This is true, but if that is all we learn from this experience, we miss its most powerful lesson. This experience is really about what faith is and what it isn't, and that we often think we have faith in God when we really don't. Surprisingly, this is a lesson many people across the world have not yet learned.

Faith is one of the most basic principles of all religious thought. In the restored gospel, the fourth article of faith lists it as the very first principle.

So what is faith? Merriam-Webster's simplest definition of faith lists it as strong belief or trust in someone or something.[1] At this most basic level, faith can be religious or secular. I can have faith that the scriptures tell me about God, and I can have faith the back of the textbook will give me the correct answers to the odd-numbered problems. As a religious believer, I can have faith my prayers reach God's ears. As a scientist, I can have faith the experiment I've set up will give valid data.

If any of the above sentences sound odd to your ears, it's just because society increasingly reserves the

---

[1] "Faith." *Learner's Dictionary*, Merriam-Webster, Incorporated, www.learnersdictionary.com, accessed 24 Nov. 2016.

word faith for religiously-themed topics. Just substitute strong belief or strong trust into any of the above sentences, and you see the definition works.

Notice we have said nothing about knowledge yet. Faith can lead to knowledge, and knowledge can lead to faith, but they are distinct. As an example, my past experience using the back of the textbook tells me it almost always gives the correct answer to the odd-numbered problems. This increases my faith, or trust, in the back of the textbook.

Knowledge and faith build upon each other. This is especially true of experiential knowledge. I had faith that God would help me find my watch. Why did I have that faith? Because of the knowledge that family members had faced similar circumstances with positive results. How did I gain this knowledge? By trusting stories my parents told me. Why did I trust them? Because of the knowledge that other stories they told were true, like the one about not touching the wood-burning stove.

We can trace all our current faith or knowledge this way, deep into the reaches of our earliest memories. This is true of both secular and religious knowledge. Why do I, as a scientist, trust this particular experiment will yield good data? Because of the knowledge my previous, similar experiments did so. What made me do my very first experiment? Trust in my college professors. What made me trust my professors? The knowledge that they taught me other things that turned out to be fairly accurate. This goes on and on down through elementary school teachers whom I trusted, which is based on faith in my parents who sent me to school.

If we would like to build a relationship with God, we must build both faith and knowledge through spiritual experience, but before we continue, let's ask a question. Why would you choose to build a relationship with God in the first place? Is he just a handy person to have around when you lose stuff? Can he put food on the table when you've lost your job? Can he explain to you all those pestering questions about theology or early church history? Can he cure your loved one's debilitating disease? Can he rescue your loved one from death? Can he save your soul?

We are told that faith in God produces miracles. So then why doesn't faith in God produce miraculous results every time? Because we often think we have faith in God when we actually don't.

I had faith God would give me my watch in ten minutes or less. I am certain my parents didn't teach me that particular time limit, but that is the lesson I learned from their stories. Notice that I didn't have faith in God, I had faith God would do something. In reality, there is rarely ever a guarantee God will do what we want, especially when we set time limits on him. I had faith in something false. Faith in a falsehood leads to what is commonly called a crisis of faith. This is a good thing. A crisis of faith tells us the thing we had faith in was not God. It was something else.

When my prayer wasn't answered in the way my faith expected, I had a crisis of faith, even if it was a relatively mild one. At that point, I had two options: stop having faith and walk away, or do some internal searching to see if my faith was a little misplaced.

In my final prayer, correcting my misplaced faith is exactly what happened, although it was too subtle for me to recognize at the time. I originally had faith God would give me my watch if I prayed hard enough or looked long enough. In my final prayer, I had faith in God, regardless of whether I got my watch back or not. I originally had faith in an outcome. At the end, I had faith in God regardless of the outcome.

How often do we think we have faith in God when we actually have faith God will act a certain way?

I can have faith God will find me a job. I can have faith God will help me put food on the table. I can have faith the early history of God's church happened a certain way, or that his modern church will act in a particular fashion. I can have faith God will cure cancer or other debilitating diseases. I can have faith God will rescue my loved one sliding rapidly toward death.

Each of these outcomes may be worthy of your faith in certain circumstances, but none of these outcomes are guaranteed. God is not in the business of making sure everyone gets their way. God is in the business of making sure everyone knows *the* way.

Faith in God, regardless of the outcome, must always be first. Afterward, if we feel God has promised us a particular outcome, then faith in that outcome is perfectly fine, because it is rooted primarily in our faith in God.

Why is this distinction so important? Because spiritual starvation happens when faith in an outcome becomes uprooted from faith in God. How often do we hear the words, "How could God do such a thing!" or how often do we think, "I had faith in you, God!" One of the favorite phrases used by detractors is, "A true God would never do such and such."

All of these phrases are symptoms of faith in an outcome that has no root in faith in God. When we say or think such things, we absolutely need a crisis of faith. This is often the only way we can recognize that our faith needs to be re-centered on God, not some event.

If you still don't recognize the importance of this distinction, consider this: when we say, "A true God would never do such and such," what are we really saying? If we invert the sentence, it reads, "I will not have faith in God unless he acts in a way I say he can act." The latter statement reeks of pride, but somehow happily conceals itself from the speaker in the former statement. When God hears such things, it must sound similar to the parent whose child says, "A true parent would never make me go to school." From a child's perspective, school might be considered torture. From a parent's truer perspective, schooling is one of the greatest gifts they can give to their child.

A parent can't guarantee their child will only have positive outcomes at school. The child will often struggle. They will probably have too much homework at some point. They will get stressed out. At some point they may be tempted to just give up and drop out.

Why do we put our children through this? Because we know all this experience will be for their good.[2]

God has a plan for you. He can't guarantee you will only have positive outcomes. You will often struggle. You will get stressed out. At some point you may even be tempted to just give up and drop out. God asks that you trust him. Trust him through the ups and downs. Trust him in your triumphs and your failures. Trust him when

---

[2] D&C 121:7-8

he seems to hide himself from you. Trust him when his arm is the only thing holding you up.

Does this mean you should have faith in God even when your entire world is falling apart in front of your eyes, and no matter how much you pray or cry or scream at God, everything comes crashing down on top of you and crushes you to dust?

Absolutely.

We begin to have faith in God when our prayers sound like, "Heavenly Father, I really, really, really, want you to take away this trial . . . but if you won't, I guess I'll try my best to be OK with that."

This is approaching God on his terms, not ours. The perfect example of this type of prayer is, "Father . . . remove this cup from me: nevertheless not my will, but thine, be done."[3]

This is true faith in God—faith powerful enough to save a soul. And every once in a while, it will also move a mountain.

---

[3] Luke 22:42

Chapter 4

A Child of God

My mother was raised on a farm in rural Utah. I was raised in that same community in a house built on Grandpa's farmland. Most of the community was made up of farmers or cowboys. I was surrounded by people who loved to hunt, ride horses, and go camping. Somehow, I ended up becoming a physicist. Part of this was due to my father being an engineer. The only crop he ever successfully raised was a house full of nerdy kids, but because of my early surroundings, I couldn't help but take some of that farm-town life into adulthood.

For example, we had a few semi-feral cats that roamed around my childhood home. Their one job was to eat the field mice. Any cat food we put out for them was only a supplement to what was supposed to be their primary diet of mice.

The only problem was these semi-feral cats were hoping for an upgrade in their social status. They would let us kids pet them if we didn't approach them too quickly, and they loved to sneak into the warm house on a cold winter night. After hiding out in all parts of the house, they would eventually get caught licking the butter plate on the table, and my dad couldn't help but borrow some cowboy vocabulary as he chased them out.

We also had a dog or two while growing up. They weren't herding dogs like most of our neighbors had. We were told their primary job was to protect us kids, even though none of our tiny dogs could have ever really protected us from much of anything, except maybe a naked mole rat.

As an adult, I now live in what most people would call a rural area, but our town has stores that are bigger than a gas station, so it isn't all that rural to me. We have a few semi-feral cats that roam the acres around our house, but our winters are mild enough that the cats are content with their status. Every once in a while, they leave a dead scorpion on the steps to remind me why I leave cat food out each night.

We also have two small dogs which we got for our kids. Sure, they probably would try to protect the kids from the many coyotes and the occasional mountain lion, but they are chihuahuas. The only real protection they could offer is time. The mountain lion might take thirty seconds to swallow each dog.

Our dogs do excel at one task. They are a great burglar alarm, or cat alarm . . . or anything bigger than a chihuahua alarm.

Our oldest son was once studying the picture wall in our house and asked why we don't have pictures of our dogs and cats up there with the rest of the family. At first, I thought he was joking, but no, he actually wanted us to put animal pictures up with our children. His reasoning was that if Mom and Dad reserved that wall for things they loved, why not put our pets up there too? Didn't we love our pets?

Yes, we love our pets, but the picture wall is not for things we love. The picture wall is reserved for the center of the family. In a very literal sense, my spouse and children are what make us a family. I would sacrifice anything and everything in an instant for any individual on that wall. The same cannot be said for my pets. If our dogs got eaten by a mountain lion, I would be sad, but I would be devastated if one of our children got killed by a mountain lion.

If sacrificing my life would save my child, I would do it without a second thought. I would not sacrifice my life, or let my children sacrifice their lives, trying to save a pet.

We all recognize the difference between children and pets. It is enshrined in our laws. Treating pets like children is considered a little eccentric, but treating children like pets is criminal.

Latter-day Saints, young and old, recognize the song *I Am a Child of God*.[1] Most of us have at least the first verse memorized. It is no mistake that one of the first doctrines we teach new members and children is that God is our father. Every doctrine of the restored gospel of Jesus Christ is either a direct derivative of, or is inseparably connected to, this doctrine. If any single doctrine can be called the essence of the gospel, this is it.

Many people, members and non-members, believe we are children of God, but comparatively few recognize the drastic ramifications of that belief. What is so drastic about the idea that God has children? Because we believe we are *literal* children of God. Our physical bodies, of course, are born from our biological parents here on Earth, but our spiritual bodies, or spirits, are actually born from God. In scientific terms, this means we are of the same species as God.

God's relationship with us is not master to pet, but parent to child. How can this be? God is far above us in so many ways. We humans scramble around on the Earth. God lives up in Heaven. We humans eat, sleep, and

---

[1] Randall, Naomi W. "I Am a Child of God" Intellectual Reserve, Inc. 1957.

eventually die. God creates things, makes unalterable decrees, and lives forever. How can we actually believe we are of the same species as God?

Doesn't the caterpillar wonder the same thing about the butterfly? Butterflies are delicate, beautiful creatures which spend their days soaring on the breeze and sipping nectar from flowers. Caterpillars are just big, hairy blobs which spend their whole lives eating, sleeping, and what looks a whole lot like dying. As the caterpillar's body slowly melts into a soup of cells inside the chrysalis, do they recognize this isn't the end? Do they realize their "death" is just the next step in their metamorphosis to a butterfly—a creature with abilities scarcely imaginable in their former life?

We are literal children of God. That means we can one day grow up to be like God in every sense of the word. Lorenzo Snow put it most eloquently when he stated, "As man now is, God once was: As God now is, man may be."[2]

The first half of this couplet is not emphasized much in our doctrine. We don't discuss it much in our classes. It is still true, as you cannot have the second half of the couplet without the first, but the factual knowledge of how it all works is not directly vital to our current state.

---

[2] Snow, Eliza R. *Biography and Family Record of Lorenzo Snow*. Salt Lake City, 1884, pg. 46. See also "The Grand Destiny of Man," *Deseret Evening News*. July 20, 1901, pg. 22.

The caterpillar is not directly concerned with the details about his butterfly mother's earlier life as a caterpillar, just as we aren't too concerned about the exact details of who God was before he became God.

Caterpillars are, on the other hand, directly concerned with the fact that they can one day become a butterfly. It is the driving factor behind everything they do, even if they are only unconsciously aware of it. In the same way, the second half of the couplet is absolutely central to everything we do on Earth, even if we are only unconsciously aware of it.

Everything I do for my children is because I want them to become upstanding adults. If you sit down and calculate it, parents spend most of their adult lives sacrificing for their children, and time isn't the only thing we are willing to sacrifice. Most parents would give their lives to save their children. What did our children do to deserve this treatment? Absolutely nothing.

I sacrifice for them when they can't do much more than gurgle or burp. I sacrifice for them when they kick and scratch or scream at me in anger. My love for them continues through the ups and downs, the successes and failures, whether they deserve it or not.

Isn't this illogical and irrational? Yes, but this is what it means to be a child as opposed to a pet. Parents sacrifice for their children even though they will not get an equal return on their investment of time and money. Parents love their children even when there is no logical reason to do so.

This is where the grace of God originates. God is patient with us in the middle of our spiritual temper tantrums. God loves us when we don't love him. God has hope in us when we have lost all hope. Like any good father, God would sacrifice his life for each and every one of us without a second thought.

Chapter 5

We Lived in Heaven

At the start of my two-year mission to Peru, my parents and a slew of siblings came to the Missionary Training Center to see me off. In those days, all the missionaries and their families were invited into a large room to watch an orientation video before saying their goodbyes. I was so excited to go on a mission; I could hardly contain myself.

At the end of the video, the missionaries were invited to exit the room through one door and their families to return to the parking lot through a series of other doors. I hugged each member of my family and then turned to the door, but another family was blocking the way. The room was set up in rows of metal folding chairs, and in my particular row, a missionary and his family were tearfully hugging and crying and hugging some more. I loved my family, but this was my mission. This was something I had been waiting for since before I could remember. Nothing was going to get in my way.

I began jumping rows of chairs in my suit, not caring if a few chairs clattered to the ground in the process. I didn't look back. I was on my mission.

By that evening, I was as homesick as they come. This was the absolute first time I had been on my own. I had accomplished many difficult tasks before, but I always had family support. That evening, I recognized how great it was to have a mom and dad during my youth: teaching, supporting, giving feedback, and yes, even lecturing. Now they were only accessible through letters. People I had leaned on and taken for granted for my entire life were gone. Something was missing.

Late that evening, the companion they put me with also got homesick. He was so homesick he vomited in a nearby trash can during class. Neither of us were expecting that particular turn of events on the first day of our mission, so we did the only sensible thing; we started laughing out loud. After laughing for a few minutes, the homesickness became bearable. In all truthfulness, the homesickness never entirely went away during the two years, but something about recognizing we were all in this together with a common purpose lightened the load a bit.

This experience is all but universal. We all have parents, teachers, or mentors we rely on in our youth.

Transitioning to adulthood means taking those lessons we've learned and figuring out a way to apply them to the messy realities of life without someone looking over our shoulder.

Parents, teachers, and mentors are important in our development. Life would be much harder if we didn't have early guidance from people who are concerned with our well-being.

We are literal children of God. God is the literal father of our spirits, and we can one day become like him. If our Heavenly Father loves us, wouldn't there have been some sort of training or mentoring before sending us off to this Earth? At the very least, there should have been an orientation video and a quick hug before our spirits entered our physical bodies.

It doesn't matter whether you believe this was a short training or an extremely long training. If you accept that you were born to God as spirits before physical birth, then you will likely accept that some rearing of our spirits must have happened.

The idea of a spiritual birth before our physical birth brings up a whole host of questions. Did we know our future earthly parents before birth? Did we know our spouse or children before birth? Did we know what country we were going to be born into? What about our socio-economic class? What about our race?

These are all factual knowledge questions for which we don't have clear answers. Luckily, none of these questions are as important as the fact that we lived with God before birth, and he gave us training on how to succeed in this life.

Why can't we remember any of this training? The answer to that question lies in another question. Why can't I remember anything that happened to me before the age of two or three? Important things happened to me in those years. I was fed, clothed, learned to communicate, and learned to love and be loved. Those years were the basis for everything later in my life. If that time was so important, why can't I remember any of it?

Memory is a function of our physical brains, and while memories are created in infancy, the function of storing memories is not yet fully developed. In fact, this function continues to develop into our teenage years. This is why adults generally retain relatively few memories from before the age of ten, even though if you ask an eight-year old what they did last week they would remember . . . well sometimes.

So why can't we remember any of our pre-earth life training? Because our physical brains didn't exist at that point. The memory of that training couldn't be stored in the neural connections of our brain, because we had no neurons yet.

Then what's the point? If our loving Heavenly Father wanted to give us some final words of advice before sending us to this big, scary, Earth, wouldn't that be important? Wouldn't it be nice to have a memory of that training? The whole point of training is to make the subsequent event easier. Well, why in the world didn't God make sure we could remember it?

He did. The memories just aren't in our physical brains.

To begin to explain where these memories lie, let's say you sit down with a random three-year-old at a table with two treats, one in front of each of you. Before the child can eat her treat, you quickly grab both treats and eat them. If the child isn't already too terrified, you will probably get a response such as, "Hey! That's not fair!"

You would even get the same response from another three-year-old who was observing but not involved with the treats at all. By taking something from someone else, you harmed them, and we all know that we aren't supposed to hurt others, even though we all admit to hurting others from time to time.

This three-year-old will probably not retain any memory of your interaction—her brain is not yet able to store memories well—but when she is an adult, she will still retain the knowledge that we aren't supposed to hurt others. If this lesson about being kind to others is not a memory stored in her brain, where is it stored? Why does every human have the same lesson stored somewhere, regardless of culture and regardless of some of our best efforts to forget it?

None of us have any physical memory of receiving the training classes where these rights and wrongs were taught, but we all know a right or wrong when we see one. They are as clear as our best physical memories.

Being kind to others isn't the only intrinsic lesson we humans possess. We all know the list of morals, even if we may have trouble describing the list in detail.

But if there is a universal morality across cultures, why is there so much disagreement about moral practices? You might think it's because people know what is right, but they just do what is wrong most of the time. This may be partially true, but it doesn't tell the whole story.

We actually have only a handful of basic moral lessons embedded in our souls. We must navigate complex moral scenarios using these relatively simple rights and wrongs.

For example, one time my two younger brothers and I were innocently playing a board game when my older brothers decided to play a trick on us.

They gave us some candy.

This may not sound like a very nasty trick, but they knew the habits and practices of sugar-starved kids. The happy scene of three kids playing a game quickly descended into a full-blown fist fight. The only reason I remember this encounter is because my older brothers filmed the whole thing. They called this particular episode, "Pigs at a Trough."

There was plenty of candy for each of us, so why did we turn to violence? Was it because one child wanted all the candy for himself? No, it was because each of us thought the candy wasn't divided equally. We turned to violence in the name of fairness. We committed a moral wrong in the name of a moral right.

When complex moral topics come up in politics, such as abortion, gay marriage, income inequality, drug use, capital punishment, etc., you never hear one side say, "Yes, I know this is morally wrong, but I don't really care." Both sides argue for their case in the name of fairness, justice, liberty, necessity, societal benefit, etc.

Slavery is currently viewed almost unanimously as a moral outrage, but a few hundred years ago, both pro-slavery advocates and abolitionists relied on moral arguments to defend or attack slavery.

This is the best evidence that there exists a basic universal morality. We all have a handful of lessons which we expect everyone else to have. When we argue for or against a particular moral practice, we build our case with the common language of these few basic morals, even if each side undoubtedly disagrees with how the other side uses them.

People feel a deep impulse to be moral; we are just quite talented at convincing ourselves that we are acting morally when we aren't. If we are careful to think deeply about our actions, though, something inside will often tell us the truth.

This fundamental drive to live according to a shared set of morals is often called our conscience. Sometimes we call it instinct, but we all recognize this is not physical memory we are talking about. This is something much deeper. This is something ingrained in our souls. This is part of what we carried with us into this life.

This spiritual memory does not just store training or lessons. Yes, we all recognize a right or a wrong when we see it, but more importantly, we recognize the teacher.

We would recognize God if we met him.

In the same way that we can't describe the training we received as a spiritual being, we can't describe in detail what God is like, because we don't have a physical memory of him. Despite this, if God were to come down and talk to us, we would immediately get the feeling that we knew him, even if he came without all the trumpets and angels. In the presence of God, our spirits would instinctively cry out to him. He is our father after all.

That first evening of my two-year mission, I wasn't homesick for the lessons my father and mother taught me; I was homesick for them. I just wanted to be in their presence. I still knew they loved me and were concerned for me—they would say as much in their letters—but I missed feeling that directly.

This is the state in which we sometimes find ourselves. Our spirits recollect all too well what it was like to be in God's presence. And even though we can't describe it in words, we periodically feel like something is missing—something we once had. No doubt our spirits took for granted how great it was to have God right there teaching, supporting, and guiding us. Yes, we can still pray to God and feel his influence in our lives, but deep down, we know it isn't the same. We yearn for the day we can return to live with him again.

We lived in Heaven a long time ago. And even though the homesickness never entirely goes away, it helps to know we are all in this together with a common purpose. And when we meet God in the next life, it won't be for the first time. It will be our homecoming.

Chapter 6

A Simulation

There is currently much talk about sending humans to Mars. Multiple countries are planning and preparing as they try to overcome the many technological and logistical hurdles for such a voyage.

One particularly fascinating problem that has received much attention is the human problem. Science and engineering may soon find a way to get humans safely out to Mars, protect them from increased radiation, mitigate the effects of prolonged weightlessness, find a way to feed them for the two years or more, and return them safely to Earth, but what about the human mind? Can humans live for years in close quarters without driving each other crazy? Will one of the crew finally crack when so-and-so with the crooked teeth "borrows" their toothbrush for the umpteenth time? What about when astronauts Bill and Sally get together, then break up, then get together again? Will mission control have to hire more psychologists than engineers?

You can train an astronaut to be physically fit, incredibly smart, and have quick reflexes, but what do you do if they are a nervous breakdown waiting to happen? Hopefully you can find that out before you actually send them to Mars.

There exist multiple Mars habitat simulators around the world. They are tiny buildings where people are kept in close quarters for long durations of time, sometimes over a year. Any country which is serious about sending humans to Mars is supporting at least one.

Some of these simulators are out in the middle of a desert, and the participants walk around the desert in full space suits. They are serious about trying to simulate the whole Martian experience in every way. Other simulators concentrate on the psychological. The longest isolation happened in the Mars-500 simulator, supported by Russia, The European Space Agency, and China. Six crew members were in complete isolation from the outside world while they simulated a trip to Mars and back lasting five-hundred and twenty days.

Three overwintering stations, one American, one Russian, and one French-Italian, located on the Antarctic plateau, also serve an interesting purpose relating to Mars exploration. Each of these stations are completely isolated during the Antarctic winter. The small crews must be completely self-sufficient, and they know if any emergency were to happen, there is zero chance of rescue. The psychological effects this has on the crews is similar to what would be required by a crew headed to Mars.

All of this is scientific fact, but let's take a step or two into science fiction. The biggest problem with these Mars habitat simulators is that each person sitting in the confined quarters knows they are not on Mars. In most cases, rescue is just minutes away. Let's say we discovered a way to alter people's memories. When we put this memory-altering substance into the air of the habitat, the crew actually forgets most of their previous life. They retain the skills necessary to accomplish their daily tasks, but each of them actually believes they are on Mars. Let's assume they each consented to this selective amnesia before their two-year mission deep in a red-rock desert somewhere, and they will regain their memories as soon as they breath untainted air again. Observers could watch their every move and grade the mental stamina of each potential astronaut. More importantly, at the end of the simulation, the crew themselves would know if they were truly cut out for the real thing. Many people think they can handle the mental strain of a difficult task beforehand, but actually going through it is another story. Wouldn't this be the ultimate simulator to test whether each member of the crew has the mental stamina it takes to complete the real-life mission to Mars?

We are literal children of God. If we are to become like our Father one day, with all the powers and abilities of a god, wouldn't it make sense for our training to include a simulator of what a god's life will be like?

Simulators expose people to the real-world conditions of a particular task while protecting themselves and others from many of the real-word dangers of that same task. We use simulators any time we give a person a new and potentially dangerous power. This is for their own safety and the safety of others. People drive on a closed course or a parking lot before they drive on a public road. People shoot on a gun range before they go hunting. Surgeons cut up cadavers before they cut into living people. Pilots sit in flight simulators before they carry hundreds of people in an airplane. If common sense tells us to use simulators in these cases, wouldn't it make sense for God to do the same?

What would a god simulator look like? It would look a whole lot like what we are all going through right now.

We are in an environment where good and evil are both present. We have an innate spiritual drive to do good, almost as if that was the whole point of this life. We have been given incredible, god-like power to practice with, specifically the power to create other lives. There are always a bunch of people around us with almost no power, no intelligence, and no way to defend themselves from our whims, specifically children and babies.

This life would really be the ultimate god simulator if our memories were altered beforehand to make it easy for us to convince ourselves we are all on our own. If we have no recollection of signing up for this god simulator, we are free to believe that this life is all there is to our existence. Isn't that also a good description of our current state? We have a spiritual memory of God and our pre-Earth training, but the memory is subtle. You might even say it is veiled. It is quite easy to ignore our conscience in the heat of the moment.

If this life is indeed a simulation of what God's life is like, then what exactly are we being graded on? How do we know if we passed?

First off, "graded" is not an appropriate word to describe the outcome of this simulation. Remember, a simulation is a way we can gain skills and test our stamina before we move on to the real thing. Therefore, this life is not really a test; it is a practice round. This life is a proving ground of sorts. We don't get a grade at the end. We gain the skills necessary to move on from the simulation into reality, along with the confidence that we are capable of handling the real thing.

So what are these skills? What are we being tested on? It is easiest to begin to understand what this life *is* testing, by explaining what this life *is not* testing.

This life is not as much a test of knowledge as it is a test of faith. Our pre-Earth life was a test of knowledge. There, we had all the facts before us, and we were asked to make the choice to come here. This life, on the other hand, is a test to see what we do when we have comparatively few facts before us. We simply cannot spend our whole life researching all the facts about God before making our decision to follow him. We must walk uncomfortably by faith, trying our best to struggle forward with confidence despite all we don't know.

This life is not as much a test of what we believe as it is a test of what we do. Many people in this life have an incorrect idea of God. I certainly had an incorrect idea of God in my youth compared with my adulthood, and my current idea of God is certain to change later in life. The fact is, none of us have a perfect understanding of God. Having a more correct idea of God certainly helps, but it does us no good if we spend our whole life believing in an above-average idea of God without doing anything about it. Our belief, even if our idea of God isn't perfect, should absolutely and completely change how we live our life.

This life is not as much a test of what we do as it is a test of who we become. We aren't here to finish some checklist of good deeds. We are here to practice using the God-like powers we already have been given.

Knowing about God is a good thing. Believing in God and doing what he asks is even better, but ultimately, we are here to become like God. All of us know what's right and wrong, and even if it seems that no one is watching or no one really cares, we are here to practice being like the God our souls are, deep down, already intimately familiar with. That can be done in the grandest cathedral in the richest country or the simplest hut in the deepest jungle. After all, God is the father of *all* of us.

Chapter 7

Perspective

I entered graduate school with a wife and a young child. At that time my perspective on life began to change. I don't know whether the realization finally caught up to me that I was more or less an adult by now, or whether it was just the strain of graduate-level physics courses. I no longer had the perspective of a child looking at the world; I had the perspective of someone who had brought a child into the world.

That perspective changes everything.

In addition, my views of religion began to change. Serious questions about God and faith began piling up. God wasn't just about knowing the correct answer in Sunday School or memorizing twenty-five verses of scripture per year. Religion was no longer a neat, little, black and white picture which made perfect sense. With my new perspective, everything that was once so simple had become entirely perplexing. My questions about church history or doctrine looked like they would never be answered.

You might call this a full-blown crisis of faith. There were many reasons why I didn't lose my testimony in the midst of all this, but the most unexpected reason was that getting a PhD in physics was causing me to go through what I call a crisis of science at the same time.

In my graduate-level physics classes, all the math and scientific assumptions were discussed in all their gory detail. Serious questions began piling up. As a youth, I had naturally assumed the textbook was always correct and scientific experts were certain about everything. Now that I was working directly with experts, and slowly becoming an expert in my particular field of research, that view was shattered. Science was no longer a neat, little, black and white picture that made perfect sense. With my new perspective, things that seemed so simple, like gravity or electric charge, were active fields of study, and in many ways entirely perplexing. Basic assumptions in science had been discovered to be completely wrong in the past, which was terribly disconcerting. My questions about the history of science or current scientific assumptions looked like they would never be answered.

A crisis of faith often feels like life just kicked your religious legs out from under you. When that happens, some people turn to the seemingly stable ground offered by science or logic. In my case, I got both my religious and scientific legs kicked out from under me at the same time. This quickly developed into a general epistemological crisis—I wasn't sure what I knew about anything anymore. My religion hadn't changed. Science hadn't suddenly become less stable, but my perspective of each had changed.

We all have these perspective altering moments throughout our lives. How many of us remember the time our parents, or a teacher, told us the sun doesn't actually rise or set, but that the Earth is rotating which just makes the sun look like it is rising or setting. Most of us remember the moment when we realized our parents weren't perfect. Some of these moments pass by without too much trouble. Others put us in crisis mode.

These same perspective altering moments happen on a large scale as well. One of the more recent changes in scientific perspective happened in the early twentieth century. Our idea of the universe was drastically different back then. We assumed it was just a big soup of stars a few hundred thousand light-years across. Along came Edwin Hubble in 1925 with the hundred-inch telescope at Mount Wilson Observatory. Hubble noticed a few Cepheid variable stars in some of those pesky spiral nebulae, or "clouds," spread all over the night sky. Luckily, he knew a way to use Cepheid variable stars to calculate their distance from Earth. Imagine what went through his mind when the first calculation was a million light-years away, far bigger than the accepted size of the universe at the time. Those weren't clouds; they were whole new "island universes," or galaxies, out beyond our own galaxy. To humanity, the universe all of a sudden got much larger.

Our telescopes look at the same night sky today, but our worldview is entirely different. Of course, this change of perspective didn't happen overnight. The discussion of island universes had been going on for multiple years in what is called the "Great Debate," but this example still stands as one of the greatest changes in scientific perspective of the twentieth century. The word "universe" after Hubble meant something quite different than it did before Hubble, just as the words "falling star" today mean something very different from the medieval idea.

So why is perspective so important in the restored gospel? Because we use the same words as other religions, but those words often mean different things to us. The words "salvation" and "Heaven" mean something different to Latter-day Saints. These differences usually aren't large but alter our perspective entirely.

For example, when Latter-day Saints say the word "God," we mean something different than other religions.

This change in perspective makes almost all atheistic arguments against God no longer applicable.

If we are literal children of God, and he himself was once in a similar state as us, then he cannot be omnipotent in the strictest, scientific sense of the word. He achieved his Godhood by following some set of requirements, and he doesn't have the power to alter those requirements. Whenever the scriptures say something must be the case or "God would cease to be God,"[1] that verse is listing one of these requirements.

If God is only all-powerful, as opposed to omnipotent, then all the arguments against God that rely on a strict definition of omnipotence do not apply to the restored gospel of Jesus Christ.

Similar arguments can be made to show God is not omniscient in the strictest sense of the word, even if he knows the "end from the beginning"[2] when it comes to this little proving ground we call Earth.

But wait, aren't we losing something by saying God is only all-powerful and all-knowing as opposed to omnipotent and omniscient? Absolutely not.

God has significantly more power than humans. So much so, that we cannot tell the functional difference

---

[1] See Alma 42:13, 22, 25 and Morm. 9:19. For other restrictions on God, see D&C 82:10, Enos 1:6, Titus 1:2, James 1:13, etc.
[2] Abr. 2:8

between all-powerful and omnipotent. Does the ant recognize the difference between being stepped on versus being crushed by the tire of an automobile? There is a real difference in force between the two, but there is no functional difference to the ant. When the caterpillar finds out the butterfly cannot fly above some altitude without dying, does that make flight any less wondrous or impossible to the caterpillar?

The question is not, "Can God do everything?" The question is, "Can God save me?" If we were stranded on a desert island, we wouldn't ask the rescue ship how many guns and missiles it was equipped with. We wouldn't pester the vessel with questions about how big a ship it could destroy or if it had enough nuclear weapons to end all civilization on the planet. We would simply ask the captain if he could save us.

Because the Latter-day Saint perspective on God does not include strict omnipotence or omniscience, along with variations on other characteristics of God, all the most common atheistic arguments, except one, do not apply to us. What is that one exception? The argument that relies on what is permissible as spiritual evidence. We discussed this argument in the first two chapters.

When I explain to atheists the concept of God in the restored gospel of Jesus Christ, the first argument they turn to is often a variation of the chicken and the egg argument. This argument states that if God created us, then something must have created God and so on down the line forever and ever. Where did it all begin?

This argument doesn't apply to the restored gospel, because at its heart, this isn't actually an argument against the existence of God. It's an argument against the idea of God as the "first mover", something which we do not believe, at least in the classical sense. For Latter-day Saints, this argument simply states that we lack knowledge about how the generation of Gods began. Is this surprising?

When we lack knowledge, it can make the question perplexing or even seem illogical. A similar, down-to-Earth question is how did the whole caterpillar/butterfly system start in the first place? Did a worm mate with a dragonfly way back in the distant past? How did the first caterpillar know to make a chrysalis and dissolve himself into a pre-butterfly soup? How could nature possibly view that as a good idea? Scientists may have sufficient knowledge to have a guess at the answer, but to the common person without knowledge, this question is completely perplexing. The whole system seems illogical. But just because we don't know how the system got started doesn't mean caterpillars and butterflies are all figments of our imagination.

I don't intend to discuss each atheistic argument and point out why it doesn't really apply to the restored gospel, but one argument which deserves further discussion is the problem of pain. This argument proposes that if God is omnipotent, omniscient, and omnibenevolent, or all-loving, why is there pain or evil in the world? Why doesn't he stop it?

This argument does not apply in the restored gospel, because God is not omnipotent or omniscient, but this doesn't tell the whole story. If God is all-powerful and all-knowing, he should still be able to extinguish some pain and evil. At the very least, he should be able to heal the child who is dying from congenital disease. Surely this is needless pain. The answer is that God is a resident of this universe along with the rest of us. We were born to him and sheltered directly in his home in Heaven, but like any parent, he knew he could not shelter us from pain and evil forever. At some point we needed to face the pain and evil of the universe. This life is a semi-protected place where God can begin to wean us from his direct protection. God did not create pain or evil, he placed us in a location where outside evil can seep in. Thus, we might one day handle the full unadulterated onslaught of what this universe can produce.

Some people view God as the labyrinth maker. He created this world with all its traps and obstacles. We succeed only if we jump through all the hoops and make it to the center of the maze.

In actuality, God is the wilderness guide. The universe is a dangerous place, filled with good and evil. He didn't create evil. He didn't even create the basic rules, but he knows where all the dangers lie. He knows how to guide us through the wilderness; and moreover, he knows how to teach us to become wilderness guides ourselves to show the next generation the only safe way.

Remember, everything we do here is preparing us to become like God. We must learn to enjoy sacrificing for others, because God sacrifices everything for us. We must learn to trust in God, because he entrusts us with his children. We must learn to suffer through pain and sorrow, because God suffers every day as he sees the choices his children make.

This perspective changes everything.

Chapter 8

I've a Mother There

Most people are familiar with electric fields and magnetic fields. Magnets are common toys for children, and who hasn't experienced a static electric shock at some point in their life?

Historically, magnets were used in compasses while electricity was considered relatively useless. Up until the early nineteenth century, electricity and magnetism were thought to be separate forces. They look different enough on the surface. If you rub a glass rod with silk, it will attract little pieces of paper. A magnet won't attract paper no matter how much you rub it, but it will attract iron nails without any rubbing at all.

It came as a bit of a shock in 1820 when scientists discovered that a nearby electric current will deflect the magnet in a compass.[1] Electricity and magnetism aren't two separate forces; they are different manifestations of the same force.

It was an even greater shock when, in 1865, James Clerk Maxwell announced to the world that if you combine an electric field and a magnetic field, you get light.[2] This is still shocking news to many non-scientists today. It goes against all our natural experience. Maxwell was saying that if you combine the thing found in compasses with the thing found in static electricity, you get light. Light is nothing like magnets or static electricity, but when you combine them, they become something new and powerful.

How could two things that seem so completely different combine into something far beyond what either one could achieve separately? This is actually relatively common in nature. Protons and Neutrons are unremarkable separately, but they can combine in various ways to form all the elements we interact with. Space and time are easy to understand separately, but when

---

[1] Oersted, Hans Christian. "Experiments of the Effect of a Current of Electricity on the Magnetic Needle." *Annals of Philosophy*. 1820, Vol. 16, p. 273-277

[2] Maxwell, James Clerk. "A Dynamical Theory of the Electromagnetic Field." *Philosophical Transactions*. Royal Society of London. 1865, 155, p. 459-512.

combined into spacetime, they create something quite complex and extraordinary.

In short, the rule of nature is often, "The whole is greater than the sum of the parts." This same rule applies directly to children of God. First, our spirits and our physical bodies are two very different things. Without our spirits, our bodies are dead. Without our bodies, our spirits cannot affect the physical realm in the same way. When united, our spirits and bodies are a unique thing with added power and ability. In many ways, the union of spirit and body turns us into something new and extraordinary.

When Joseph Smith first saw God, he was shown that God has a physical body. He was later told that a physical, resurrected body was a necessary part of what made God who he was.[3] We can assume that at least part of God's power comes from his perfect unity between body and spirit. The unifying of spirit and body is more than the sum of the parts.

The second way this rule of nature applies to us as literal children of God can be stated in a question: If we are to become like God one day, what does that mean for women? Society generally assumes God is male. Up to now, I have exclusively used the pronoun "he" to describe

---

[3] See D&C 130:22 and D&C 93:33

him, but if our Heavenly Father has literal children, doesn't reason say we have a Heavenly Mother as well? Would the title "God" apply to her also? The answer is yes, because in the same way light needs two components to be light, she is part of what makes our Heavenly Parents our God. Part of the reason God seems so different than us is because God is not an individual. God is a couple. When an eternal man is paired with an eternal woman, and they become perfectly united, something new and powerful is made. They are God.[4]

Yes, an individual can receive great power from God. A person can even receive enough power and authority from God to become part of the Godhead, a sort of partnership with God that comes with the title "God" by proxy, but a full God must be capable of having spirit children. An individual can never do this. A man can never be God in the fullest sense of the word unless he is paired with a woman, and a woman can never be God unless she is paired with a man.[5]

Wouldn't it be nice to have a word which described this better? In English, the word God is always singular. In ancient Hebrew, the word for God, Elohim, is always plural. In the restored gospel of Jesus Christ, we have co-

---

[4] See D&C 132:19-20
[5] See D&C 132:15-17

opted the word Elohim to apply to God, and the plural meaning of the word is sometimes explicitly intended. Thus, the word Elohim could apply to our Heavenly Parents, both the Father and the Mother. This simply isn't captured in the word God.

This brings up a question. When we pray to God, who are we really praying to, the Father or the Mother?

When I call my parents on the phone, it doesn't matter who answers, they both listen in on the conversation. When I'm having an important discussion with one of them, they will often just put the phone on speaker mode or hold it in such a way that they can both hear and respond equally. This is because they both love me and are both interested in what I do.

When we pray to God, both the Father and the Mother are listening. This is something we have no control over. They both love us, and they are both interested in what we have to say.

Should we ever pray to the Mother exclusively? Probably not. What would happen if I called my mother and said, "Hey, Mom, something really important happened to me, but I don't want you to tell Dad about any of it." Apart from my father being offended, since he is already listening in on the conversation, my mother would likely refuse to take part in the secrecy. My parents are close. They share everything.

Our Heavenly Parents are closer. Their perfect unity is what makes them God. In a very literal way, if ever we try to consciously exclude one Heavenly Parent from the other, we are no longer dealing with God. If we were to extract the electric field out of light, we wouldn't be dealing with light anymore.

When we begin our prayers with the words, "Our Heavenly Father," both the Father and the Mother are listening. Both the Father and the Mother can respond equally. Neither of them has any ego that needs to hear their own title at the beginning of a prayer. There is no competition between the two. When we begin a prayer, our Parents are simply happy we called home.

This is the type of relationship we should strive for in our own marriages. The already impossible task of making our thoughts, words, and deeds God-like, is actually doubly impossible. Not only must we become like God as individuals, but also as couples.

This brings up another question. If God must be a couple, what about those who never marry in life, or after an honest attempt have a failed marriage? The simple answer is that they have the opportunity to marry sometime after death. Does this thought make living a single life easy? Of course not. Does this mean single people can just put off learning how to be unified with others until after life? Absolutely not. Becoming unified is a vital part of why we are here on Earth. If we are never able to marry, or had a failed marriage, we must still learn to be unified with others. Marriage is not required to learn how to work together in a just cause. Yes, marriage may give you more opportunities to practice unity, but we are all required to learn how to be perfectly united with others.

Another question this topic brings up is if God must be a couple, why can't God be two men or two women? While we don't know all the factual knowledge behind the answer to this question, we do know the answer.

"The Family: A Proclamation to the World," a doctrinal statement signed by the First Presidency and Quorum of the Twelve Apostles, says that "Gender is an essential characteristic of individual, premortal, mortal, and eternal identity and purpose."[6] It is tempting to think this is a novel doctrine found only in this document. In reality, it is simply a restatement of the doctrine of Heavenly Parents with a simple added assumption. Doctrine and Covenants section 132 states that God must be a man and a woman.[7] If we accept this fact, then the simple assumption is that there must be something

---

[6] "The Family: A Proclamation to the World." The Church of Jesus Christ of Latter-Day Saints. 1995, para. 2.
[7] See D&C 132:15-17, 19-20

complementary about the male and female gender. I'm not speaking of variation in personalities we often see in men and women. To be complementary on this scale, there must be something fundamentally different between men and women, which then sometimes leads to personality variations.

The most obvious complement between spiritual genders is that when combined, they are able to have spiritual children. We don't know how spirits are birthed, but it most likely doesn't include physiological reproduction or physical carrying of the spirit in the womb. What we do know is that an individual cannot have spirit children, nor can two males, nor two females.

If we accept that we have Heavenly Parents, then the simplest explanation to account for this is the idea that gender is not exclusive to our physical body, but is an essential characteristic of our soul. Male and female are two entirely different manifestations of spirits that can combine into something much greater than the sum of the parts.

Combining electric and magnetic fields produces light. If we try to combine two electric fields, they can modify the overall electric field strength or completely cancel each other out, but pairing two electric fields simply will never create light.

Accepting the doctrine of Heavenly Parents means accepting that marriage is between a man and a woman. What does this mean for gay Latter-day Saints? Is there a place in God's plan for them? Absolutely. God is the father of all us of us.

How exactly does this work? If becoming God is strictly for a male and female, do gay people become straight in Heaven, or do they simply have spirits that mismatched their physical gender in life? God hasn't given us the answer to these questions yet. But if he hasn't given us the answer, why does he require gay people to live a seemingly impossible celibate life? If this requirement is in fact impossible, it would be just another impossibility perched on our ever-growing stack. God seems to be in the habit of asking the impossible.

For those who do marry, how do a husband and wife go about the impossible task of becoming perfectly united? For those who don't marry, how does a person become united with others? And how do we know when we are successful?

On my two-year, LDS mission, I served alongside multiple companions. In our mission, there was always a senior companion and a junior companion. The senior companion was technically "in charge", but my mission president made it absolutely clear this was in name only. He took seriously the scripture, ". . . he that is greatest among you shall be your servant."[8] It was common practice for my mission president to ignore seniority when assigning missionaries as senior and junior companions. I served the last few months of my mission as junior companion to missionaries who hadn't even been out a year yet.

A common refrain my mission president would drill into us went something like this, "You are united as a missionary companionship when someone asks you who the senior companion is, and it genuinely takes you a moment to remember."

A similar concept applies to a marriage. We don't divide the family into various departments and ignore everything except our accepted responsibilities. We work together in all aspects of family life, even if one or the other of us takes the natural lead in specific areas. We don't alternate days as to which spouse is "in charge." No one is strictly in charge, and all major decisions are made unanimously.

We are on the path to unity as a couple when there is discussion but no argument, accepting of each other's ideas but no coercion. If someone asks us, "Who wears the pants in the marriage?" it genuinely takes us a moment to realize they aren't talking about clothing, because we

---

[8] Matt. 23:11

honestly don't remember the last time there was any power struggle.

There is no such thing as power struggle with our Heavenly Parents. Both were involved in the creation of this world, even if one or the other took the natural lead in specific areas of that creation. The Father and Mother both watch and worry over their children. They both rejoice at our meager successes and weep with us in our sorrows. They encourage, they reprimand, they teach, and they bless. In short, they are our parents.

The Heavenly Father and Mother are perfectly united in such a way that it is difficult to tell them apart. And this is the goal. A husband and wife are united when you finish each other's thoughts. You are united when you aren't exactly sure where your soul ends and your spouse's begins.

To become like God, we must become God-like as individuals and couples. If we are unable to marry in this life, we still must learn to be unified with others as we look forward to the day when marriage will be possible. How do we go about accomplishing this long list of impossibilities? Frankly, we can't do it. It's impossible. We would need an infinite amount of help.

This infinite help is the topic of the next section.

PART TWO

Christ

Chapter 9

An Atonement

One evening, as we sat down for family dinner, our conversation started off something like this:

"You don't care if I live or die!" my young son screamed at me.

I rubbed the bridge of my nose. "I didn't say that. I just said you need to clean up your lunch dishes before you get dinner."

My son flopped on the floor. "I'm starving to death! I can't even feel my legs."

"Look, if you ever want to be a grown-up, you're going to have to clean up after yourself. You will probably even have to learn to clean up after other people."

"Which is more important, clean dishes or me dead?"

I would like to say these sorts of episodes are extremely rare, but like all parents know, and prefer not to advertise, this is fairly common.

Like most parents, my wife and I try to help our children in every way we can. We love our children and want them to reach their full potential. The trouble is, our help isn't always wanted or appreciated. Asking the kids to turn off a video game and play outside is often perceived as Dad not wanting anyone to have any fun. Asking to clean a room is perceived as downright slavery.

This is a problem of perspective. If my children truly understood my hopes for them, or at least trusted my methods a little more, they would likely be more receptive to my help—the kind of help that doesn't just give them what they want, but prepares them for what's coming down the road.

Of course, just because my children's problems might seem silly to adult ears doesn't mean those problems aren't distressing to them. Trouble is defined not by comparing it to other people's trouble but by how much distress it causes the individual going through it.

We all have trouble in life. Sometimes this trouble is of our own making. Other times it is pushed on us by events outside our control. All trouble, large or small, causes varying levels of distress. We can sometimes overcome these trials primarily on our own, but we've all been in a predicament so overwhelming that we have no choice but to ask for outside help.

Some of the most common, and often most difficult, problems life can throw at us are financial hardship, marital strife, and terminal disease or death. It is, therefore, no mistake that the most common analogies for the atonement involve overcoming debt,[1] reconciliation of relationships,[2] and reversing disease or death.[3] This is another way of saying the atonement overcomes the most difficult problems in life.

But if the atonement is this simple, why do none of these analogies seem to capture it fully? And more importantly, why is the atonement so hard to understand in the first place? If the atonement is so vital to our salvation, why does it have to be so perplexing? The answer is because it is an infinite atonement.[4] It is everything to everyone, and as anyone who has studied mathematics knows, infinity is difficult to understand. It is a concept different from every other concept and therefore, must be treated differently.

This doesn't mean we should give up on ever understanding the atonement. We can still understand the infinite atonement, at least in as much as it affects the rest of the equation.

---

[1] See, for example, Acts 20:28 or Matt. 18:21-35
[2] See, for example, Eph. 5:23-25
[3] See, for example, Isa. 53:4-5 or Mal. 4:2
[4] See Alma 34:10

Let's begin by understanding what sort of trouble the atonement is trying to help us with. The scriptures say the atonement allows us to "escape from the grasp of that awful monster . . . death and hell."[5] Isaiah says, "he hath borne our griefs and carried our sorrows,"[6] which seems to imply the atonement can alleviate our suffering. Another verse says, "be perfected in him."[7] This list is not all-inclusive, but it hits the major items affecting us. Who wouldn't be happy if they suffered less, became perfected, and were pulled from the jaws of death and hell?

This brings up an interesting question. Why do we have all this trouble anyway? If death and hell are so monstrous, why did an all-powerful God let the monster out of the cage in the first place? Why would a loving parent let their children loose with a monster on the prowl? Because we are literal children of God, and we are here to become like him. If you want to become a lion tamer, at some point you are going to have to face a real-life lion. God has complete power over death and hell. If we are to become like God, how do we expect to gain that same power without ever facing the terrible monster ourselves?

---

[5] 2 Ne. 9:10
[6] Isa. 53:4-5
[7] Moro. 10:32

This Earth was created, Adam and Eve fell, and death and sin were allowed into the world, along with a healthy dose of suffering. All this was in the original plan. Death, sin, or anything else that can stop us from becoming like God must be mastered. Being like God is what perfection is all about. A God must live forever, so if we want to be like God, we must overcome death. A God can never sin, which is defined as ungodly behavior, so if we want to become like God, we must never sin. A God must continue on under extreme suffering; so must we.

Thus, we see that no matter which particular troubles we have in life, there is actually only one trouble we face. Every item on the complete list of troubles which the atonement helps us with is just a symptom of this one, underlying problem: We are literal children of Heavenly Parents, and we are here to become like them in every sense of the word—an impossible task.

Which brings up another important question. Why is becoming like God an impossible task? Couldn't he have designed a system that was easier? Why did God set us up for failure? The answer is he didn't set us up for failure, because as we discussed before, God didn't set up this system. God is helping us follow the same path he took when he became God.

Still, if a caterpillar doesn't need outside help to become a butterfly, why is it impossible for us to become like our Heavenly Parents? Shouldn't this whole process just happen in a natural way without trying too hard?

If you think about it, overcoming the impossible to become like our parents is completely natural. A juvenile of a species who has no hope at becoming an adult without outside help is exactly the situation of our own children.

Human babies are utterly and completely helpless at birth. If a mother is unable, or unwilling, to carry the child to term, the baby will die without immediate medical intervention. Even in a normal, full-term birth, if no one is there to shelter the baby from the elements, she will die within a few hours. If no one is there to feed her, she will starve to death within a week or so. If no one will protect her from violence or treat any accidental injuries, she may die at any moment. It is literally impossible for a human child to grow into an adult without some form of outside help.

This outside help isn't temporary or small either. Raising a human child to adulthood requires massive effort and almost constant investment over many years.

In our quest to become like God, the same holds true. Our Heavenly Parents put forth massive and continual effort toward their children. We have passed the stage of development where Mother or Father must constantly hold our hand. This Earth is the equivalent to when a mother takes her child, stands them up on their wobbly legs, and points them to their father's outstretched arms a few feet away. We are on Earth taking our first steps on our own. It's no wonder most of us immediately fall flat on our faces. The atonement is our parents picking us up when we fall.

Note that we aren't talking about grace here. Webster's original 1828 dictionary defines grace as "the free unmerited love and favor of God, the spring and source of all the benefits men receive from him."[8] The atonement has its source in God's grace,[9] and God's grace has its source in the fact that we are literal children of God, but the atonement is not the same thing as grace.

This is a simple, three-step cause and effect process. God has children. God loves them. God wants to help them reach their full potential.

In a similar way, I have young children who receive my unmerited love and favor. I love my children when they clean up their dishes, and I love them when they throw their dishes on the floor and scream in my face . . . not that this has ever happened, of course.

Because I love my children, I want to help them receive joy and happiness in life by reaching their full

---

[8] "Grace." *American Dictionary of the English Language*. New York, 1828.
[9] See John 3:16

potential as an upstanding member of society who will likely have their own children one day. The help I give my children isn't always wanted or appreciated. If it were up to my children, the best help I could ever give them would be to make sure they could spend all day playing video games and eating junk food. They just don't have a good perspective on what adulthood means, so it is difficult for them to see why encouraging them to do chores could ever be seen as help.

The same holds true for our limited perspective on what it means to be like God. When we pray to God for happiness and success, why does he so often respond by giving us financial hardship? When we pray to have closer ties to spouse or family, why does God so often respond with a trial that causes marital or familial strife? When we pray for God to give new life to a deteriorating loved one, why does he so often respond by taking them home?

Why is help from God so easily mistaken for a curse from God? Because the atonement doesn't give us what we want, the atonement molds us into what *he* wants.[10]

When we fall flat on our face, the atonement is our parents picking us up to kiss our scraped nose. Then the

---

[10] Jer. 18:1-6

atonement is our parents standing us right back up again for another try.

The atonement comforts us, but it does not shelter us from the uncomfortable. The atonement absolves us from sin, but it does not free us from temptation. The atonement can overcome death, but we will all first come to know, in a most intimate manner, the awful effects of that old monster.

In short, the atonement is a word which contains everything our Heavenly Parents do for each of us, individually, to help us in our quest to be completely and utterly changed from our current state into someone like them. No wonder it is infinite.

Chapter 10

The Savior

Brain-computer interfaces have advanced significantly over the last few decades. The field had its origins in the late 1800s and early 1900s when scientists discovered that the human brain uses electricity to function.

In the 1950s, 1960s, and 1970s, scientists experimented with electrically stimulating the cochlear nerve which connects the ear to the brain. By the 1980s, a device could be implanted into the cochlea which gave some hearing to the deaf.

In the 1980s and 1990s, scientists used a similar process to bypass faulty eyes and give limited sight to the blind by directly stimulating the retina or optic nerve.

The cochlear implant and the visual prosthesis might be the most exciting cases of neural prosthesis, but other examples include allowing quadriplegics to control robotic arms and even treating Parkinson's disease or depression with deep brain stimulation. Implanting electrodes in the brain for deep brain stimulation can result in side effects: personality changes, hallucinations, and depression, to name a few. This is because altering our brain patterns can, in many ways, fundamentally change who we are. When using brain stimulation to treat depression or other psychological maladies, fundamental change is the goal.

In the past few decades, electroencephalograms (EEGs) have been used in a more general, brain-computer interface. These devices use electrodes in a helmet or swimming cap to measure your brainwaves and interpret your general mental state. The technology has advanced enough that we can now go to a store and buy the first crude devices which let you control simple toys or basic video games with your mind.

These devices aren't just for entertainment. It looks as if in the very near future, brain-computer interfaces will be used to read more complex thought patterns, such as which word you might be contemplating.

People in advanced stages of amyotrophic lateral sclerosis (ALS) are completely cut off from the outside world, almost as if they are in a coma. Now, they have begun to communicate with loved ones using a simpler form of this potential device.[1]

All of this is scientific fact, but let's take a step or two into science fiction.

Let's suppose a device is invented that can read your brainwaves and transmit them, quite accurately, directly to another person's brain. It extracts the signal and sends the raw thought data to this person. If you are happy, he directly experiences that happiness. If you are in pain, he directly experiences that pain.

Let's also assume this individual can send some of his thoughts into your brain as well. He is adept enough with this device that he can actively alter your mental state. If you are agitated, he could calm you. If you are a disagreeable sort of character, he could actively alter your personality. He could even alter your brain patterns so that any thought he planted into your brain would seem to be an idea of your own invention.

How many people would actually use such a device? Most people would never consent to use it unless they were connected to someone they trusted absolutely.

---

[1] Chaudhary U, Xia B, Silvoni S, Cohen LG, Birbaumer N. "Brain-Computer Interface-Based Communication in the Completely Locked-In State." PLoS Biology. 15(1): e1002593. https://doi.org/10.1371/journal.pbio.1002593. 2017. Note that this study used functional near infrared spectroscopy instead of EEGs.

In a very real way, you would be handing over the power to change your personality, your behaviors, and even your fundamental character.

Isn't this brain-to-brain connection just a description of our potential relationship to God? God has complete access to our thoughts, our memories, and our feelings. Because of this, he understands us perfectly. This connection can go both ways if God chooses. He can implant his thoughts and feelings into our brain, even if we don't often grasp the full details of what he is trying to communicate to us.

Not only can God communicate with us, he can fundamentally alter who we are. He can give peace to an agitated soul, or he can agitate us to get off our backside and do something. God has the power to force us to do anything he wants, and he could mask it in such a way that it would seem to us like we came up with the idea. It would even be possible to force everyone to never sin.

This path would have destroyed our agency.[2] God has given us our agency and promised never to use this power to alter us against our will. He didn't want us to become merely extensions of his own mind, he wanted us to learn and grow into our own selves.

---

[2] See Moses 4:1-4

We are children of God who are trying to become like him—an impossible task if left to our own ability. But we aren't left to our own ability; we are connected to God. Contrary to what you might think, this connection to God is not always pleasant. God's primary purpose is to fundamentally change who we are. Our first instinct is to resist change. This is why faith is the first principle of the gospel.[3] He won't change who we are without our wanting that change, and we won't want that change until we trust him. How much trust we place in God is directly related to how much change he can affect in us.[4]

Our Heavenly Parents aren't the only ones with this sort of intimate access to our souls. They chose to grant this access to another individual in an effort to save us all.

Jesus Christ, the savior of mankind, was sinless, and even though he was mortal, he was the only begotten of the Father. He could thus bear such access to each of us, along with the power granted from the Father to save us.[5]

In the Garden of Gethsemane, when Christ demonstrated his willingness, God began the process of the atonement by stretching Christ's soul across the infinite divide and attaching him to each of us. In a way

---

[3] See A. of F. 4
[4] See, for example, Alma 5:12 (10-15)
[5] See Hel. 5:11

that transcends time beyond our understanding, Christ was given access to the soul of every individual who had ever lived on the Earth, everyone who was living on the Earth at that time, and every single person who would yet be born until the end of the Earth.

We sometimes call this connection the "light of Christ."[6] If we allow it, he can fundamentally alter who we are. He can help us as we strive to become like God. Christ can change us.

In that small garden on the side of an inconspicuous hill, the man who had not yet tasted the pains of death now directly felt the pain and sorrow of all of us. The man who had never sinned now felt the wrenching consequences of innumerable spiritual deaths. The man who was "despised and rejected of men"[7] now bore the burdens of all humanity, and the infinite weight drew "great drops of blood"[8] from "every pore."[9]

Through this most intimate of all connections, Christ saw the deepest, darkest corner of our hearts, and what did he do? He planted hope.

---

[6] See Moro. 7:15-19 and D&C 84:46
[7] Isa. 53:3
[8] Luke 22:44
[9] D&C 19:18

Chapter 11

Sin's Consequence

God has given us the gift of the atonement, but Jesus Christ is the one who delivers that gift to us personally. This brings up a question. Why couldn't God be both the giver and deliverer of the gift? Why did he have to involve Christ?

The answer to this question should be clear now that we have discussed the objective of the atonement. All too often, people think the objective of the atonement is to get us into Heaven, but this is only partly true.

When I returned from my mission, I was excited to come home. Coming home meant eating my mother's home-cooked meals and talking and laughing together with family. Coming home did not mean just entering my parent's house. If my family had moved while I was on a mission, I would have come home to their new house.

In a similar way, the atonement doesn't get us into a place called Heaven. The atonement returns us to God.

The atonement reconciles us with God by cleansing us and perfecting us. Heaven is wherever our Heavenly Parents are located.

The scriptures define spiritual death as separation from God.[1] God can't come down and give us the gift of the atonement personally, because we need the atonement before we can overcome spiritual death and enter the presence of God.

To illustrate this concept, let's look at the Aviation Survival Technicians of the United States Coast Guard, commonly known as rescue swimmers. These are the men and women who are lowered from helicopters into the open ocean to rescue people before they drown—sometimes in freezing water, under severe storm, and in the pitch black of night.

Such was the case during the sinking of the *Alaska Ranger* fishing vessel off the coast of Alaska in the early hours of March 23, 2008.

At about 2:30 a.m., in a heavy storm, the ship began taking on water. By shortly after 4:30 a.m., the fishing vessel rolled to one side, slipped under the water, and deposited its forty-seven crew members into the icy water. Half of the crew managed to struggle into two life rafts, desperately trying to keep warm in the snow squalls

---

[1] See, for example, Alma 42:9 and Hel. 14:16-17

and heavy freezing spray of the twenty-foot waves. The rest of the crew were left floundering directly in the 32°F water. Some of the emergency suits, which were designed to keep water away from the body, had been torn and quickly filled with gallons of freezing water.

The first Coast Guard helicopter arrived at 5:00 a.m., about thirty minutes after the sinking of the vessel. The helicopter crew lowered their rescue swimmer into the icy deep and began to hoist survivors up one at a time. After almost an hour of slow and desperate work, they filled the helicopter with a dozen victims and had to ferry them back to the quickly approaching rescue ship.

The second Coast Guard helicopter arrived at 6:20 a.m., still pitch black at Alaskan latitudes in this season. The victims had been in the water for almost two hours at this point, near the edge of human survival in such conditions. The smaller helicopter could only hold four survivors. The rescue swimmer volunteered to stay behind so a fifth survivor could take his place while he waited with three others in a separate emergency life raft. They waited an hour for the first helicopter to return and rescue them at 8:30.

Another fishing vessel, the *Alaska Warrior*, collected the survivors from the life rafts and pulled from the water the four bodies of the captain, the chief engineer, and two other crew members. In all, forty-two were rescued, four died, and one body was never found.[2]

In this example, the helicopter represents God. The helicopter was there to rescue the crew members, but they were in a location where helicopters simply could not go. If the pilot tried to hover next to the survivor, just above the surface of the ocean with twenty-foot waves, the helicopter would crash and likely kill the survivor in the process.

The rescue swimmer acts as an intermediary between the survivor and the helicopter. He is directly attached to the helicopter, and he attaches the survivor directly to himself. At that point, the helicopter can hoist them both up.

So, what exactly stops God from coming to us directly? Sin itself is the reason.

When Moses asked to see the glory of God, God's response was, "Thou canst not see my face: for there shall no man see me, and live."[3] Doctrine and Covenants section eighty-four first discusses ordinances, priesthood,

---

[2] United States Coast Guard. "Investigation into the circumstances surrounding the sinking of the uninspected fish processing vessel *Alaska Ranger* official number 550138, in the Bearing Sea on 23 March 2008 with the loss of four lives and one person missing." Dec 20 2010, www.uscg.mil/history/docs/marinesafety/AlaskaRanger2008.pdf, pgs. 19-30, accessed Dec 1, 2016.
[3] Ex. 33:20

and the "power of godliness" and then states, "For without this no man can see the face of God, even the Father, and live"[4] Another scripture says, "For no man has seen God at any time in the flesh, except quickened by the Spirit of God. Neither can any natural man abide the presence of God . . ."[5]

Sin itself is what stops us from entering the presence of God, and it's not like God just doesn't like sinful people. It appears as if his presence would seriously harm us in some way. I don't know whether this harm actually involves us burning out in a flash of fiery ash, or whether entering the presence of God just destroys our ability to have faith, which terminates our probationary period prematurely with our sins still intact. Either way, if we had the opportunity to enter God's presence without first being cleansed and changed, we would prefer that the mountains and rocks "Fall on us, and hide us from the face of him that sitteth on the throne."[6]

Christ was sinless. He could enter God's presence of his own accord. There was nothing stopping him from walking straight up to God with his head held high. He never even had to look back . . . except that he did. He looked back on all of us. He looked on all the rest of God's

---

[4] D&C 84:22
[5] D&C 67:11-12
[6] Rev. 6:16, see also Alma 12:14

children, his brothers and sisters, who had no hope to ever stand where he stood.

We are all floundering in an ocean of sin. Reaching God on our own is as impossible as a shipwrecked victim leaping from the ocean and flying through the air to safety. But that is exactly what can happen when we allow Christ to attach himself to us. Christ is the anchor point where God's Plan of Salvation attaches in order to lift his children up to exaltation.

Chapter 12

Hope Born of Repentance

My five-year-old son, Timmy, is supremely talented in the art of the tantrum. He has an inborn sense of timing. It may be at midnight in a crowded hotel. It may be the exact moment a younger sister is blowing out birthday candles for the camera, or it may be thirty seconds after that point in the evening when the bedtime battles begin to subside and one or both parents finally sit down for what seems like the first time that evening.

If tantruming were a professional sport, Timmy would have a long and illustrious career ahead of himself. Luckily, as far as the mental health of his parents go, it looks like he might be growing out of his tantrums, even if he sometimes likes to relive the glory days.

During one particular tantrum, I was carrying him out of the room in order to minimize the damage to both person and property, while at the same time deflecting flying fists and feet. As I turned a corner, I tripped over a laundry basket, and we both went flying. I was able to catch myself, but unfortunately, the corner caught him.

As soon as he saw the blood dripping from his eyebrow, he became hysterical. I tried to get a closer look at the wound, but he turned and ran away. This was partly because he was still in tantrum mode, but also because he didn't know about the laundry basket. He thought I had purposefully slammed his face into the corner of the wall.

It took many minutes, and many drops of blood, before I could convince him to stop running from me, so I could clean the wound and examine it.

When he finally calmed down, I was ready to give him the fiery lecture he deserved, but when I saw the pain and fear in his eyes, the only thing I could say was, "Finally . . . now I can help you."

I examined the wound and thought he might need stitches at the hospital. With the mention of stitches and hospital, more hysteria ensued. I tried to reason with him, to bribe him, and to pressure him. He flat out refused to go to the hospital to see if he needed stiches. I did everything short of physically picking him up and forcing him into the car. After all, picking up and carrying a tantruming five-year-old was what got us in the mess in the first place.

After what seemed like thirty minutes or more, he finally allowed me to put on a butterfly bandage.

We often approach repentance in the same way Timmy approaches wound care. How often do we deflect the blame for our sins? How often are we paralyzed by fear of the pain involved in restitution or confession? How often do we run away from repentance in outright spiritual hysteria?

What is it that makes repentance so scary? A lack of eternal perspective.

If you were to break an arm, you would go to a doctor. This is because you understand what can happen if you don't get medical attention. Yes, it may be painful. Yes, it may be embarrassing, but if you don't seek medical attention, you run the risk of losing the function of your arm. This is the proper perspective.

If we had an eternal perspective, repentance would always be the natural choice, because we would understand the serious consequences of allowing sin to fester. When it comes to an eternal perspective, though, we all start out like little children who just don't see the big picture.[1] As we grow in the gospel we begin to see better, but if we aren't careful, we can change from the perspective of a little child to the perspective of a teenager.

---

[1] See D&C 50:40 and 1 Cor. 13:11

As all parents of teenagers understand, when a child begins to learn a little, they can sometimes be worse off, depending on their attitude.[2] A child who knows nothing will often turn to their parents. A child who feels like they already know everything will sometimes turn away from their parents.

So, what exactly is repentance? It is no more or less than turning to the Savior and following his prescription. Because of this, repentance can take many forms. The Savior's prescriptions are individually tailored.

Repentance isn't only for sins. If we continue with the medically themed examples, we could say repentance not only heals and cleanses us from sin, but it can also increase our spiritual health. If you were to seriously injure yourself, you would go to a doctor and follow their prescription, but we also go to doctors when we aren't seriously injured. If you were feeling a little off but weren't sure what was wrong, you would probably go to a doctor and follow their prescription. If we are serious about our health, we should even get periodic checkups when we think we are perfectly healthy.

A few years ago, I got a routine blood test done. I felt perfectly healthy and had no real reason to get it done. When the results came back, one number was slightly off.

---

[2] See 2 Nep 9:28-29

I went to a competent doctor, and she had me do various tests as a precaution. It seemed a little silly, but I trusted that she knew what she was doing.

To make a long story short, I was diagnosed with thyroid cancer and had a complete thyroidectomy a few months later. Because the cancer was diagnosed far earlier than normal, I will likely have no debilitating effects. If I would have waited to see a doctor until I actually felt sick, I don't know if I could say the same.

You might say the purpose of doctors is to make sick people well and to make those who are well even more healthy. Repentance is similar. David O. McKay said, "The purpose of the gospel is . . . to make bad men good and good men better, and to change human nature."[3]

Most of us understand that repentance is for when we sin or if we are otherwise spiritually ill. What we don't often realize is that repentance is also for when we think we are perfectly fine. Turning to the Savior is a good idea regardless of whether we think we need to or not. If we are filled with festering sin, he can cleanse us. If we are

---

[3] Richards, Franklin D. "Conference Report." The Church of Jesus Christ of Latter-day Saints. Oct. 1965, 136-137. See also McKay, David O. "Conference Report." The Church of Jesus Christ of Latter-day Saints. Apr. 1954, 26.

relatively clean and pure, he can concentrate on changing our nature. It's a little like incandescent light bulbs.

Incandescent light bulbs work by passing electricity through a resistive filament, which heats up to high enough temperatures to emit light. Tungsten is the metal of choice for filaments. In its pure form, it has the highest melting point of any metal. Of course, if it is not pure, then this is not the case, and when electricity is applied, it will melt and burn out. If we are not pure, we simply cannot become like God without the spiritual equivalent of burning out.

Pure tungsten is necessary, but it isn't enough, as early scientists discovered. Tungsten is a brittle metal and essentially impossible to stretch into fine enough wires for use in light bulbs. The crystalline structure of tungsten just makes it too difficult to mold into the required shape. This problem is so insurmountable that the first light bulbs used carbonized paper or bamboo as filaments. They were quite a bit dimmer and burned out quickly, but at least they could be formed into the proper shape.

In 1910, William Coolidge invented a process to make pure tungsten malleable enough to stretch into fine wire.[4] He probably didn't recognize it at the time, but his

---

[4] Coolidge, William. "Tungsten and method of making the same for use as filaments of incandescent electric lamps and for other purposes." Pat No. US1082933 A, Dec 30, 1913.

processing fundamentally changed the crystalline structure of the metal. After processing, the tungsten could be both pure enough, and malleable enough to be shaped into the correct form for a bright, long-lasting filament.

In order to enter the presence of God, not only must we be pure and free from sin, but we must have our very natures changed. We must be made malleable enough for the Lord to shape us into something completely different. Repentance is the process that cleans us and changes us. The scriptures sometimes describe this process as the Lord giving us a new heart.[5]

Yes, repentance can seem painful or difficult. Fear of the Lord and his prescribed changes can make us want to run away screaming, but running around with spiritual wounds doesn't help us any more than it did for Timmy's bleeding eyebrow.

In this life we spend far too much time running away from Christ and toward sin—or toward our own idea of what life should be. When Christ asks us to come unto him, we are afraid of him, because we think ripping out our stony heart and giving us a new heart of flesh will hurt far worse than just hunkering down with our current pain.

---

[5] Ezek. 36:25-27

When you muster enough faith to trust in the Lord and turn to him, you shouldn't be surprised when he doesn't begin the long lecture we all deserve, but simply says, "Finally . . . now I can help you."

Chapter 13

Where Is Heaven?

I enjoy road trips. At least once a year we squeeze the kids into the van, already filled with luggage, and drive the seven hundred miles to Grandma's and Grandpa's house. The fact that we continue to do this despite the twelve hours of driving in one day with countless potty breaks, feeding breaks, diaper breaks, and sanity breaks, must mean I enjoy road trips, right?

I'm not exactly sure why I enjoy them. It probably has something to do with the scenery, and I'm sure it has much to do with the destination, but I think I also just enjoy driving. There is something about traveling seven hundred miles while only having to move my foot an inch or two against the gas pedal and twisting my hands no more than a few feet around the circumference of a wheel. I do this while sitting in a comfortable chair, eating loads of junk food, and listening to audiobooks loud enough to drown out the periodic screaming in the seats behind me.

Let's say someone were to ask me what it was that got me past the seven hundred miles to my destination: the vehicle or my hands and feet that operated it? The question is silly. It isn't one or the other, but both. If I have a well-functioning vehicle but never use my hands or feet to operate it, I would go nowhere. If I were to sit on a chair in my house while moving my foot a few inches and twisting my hands in a circle, I also would go nowhere. If I want to reach my destination, I need a vehicle, and I need to operate it correctly.

This answer should be clear to anyone who has travelled in an automobile, but the same answer applies to an age-old theological question which often isn't quite so clear: is it our faith that saves us, or is it our works? The deceptively simple answer is both save us.

The atonement of Jesus Christ takes our meager works and multiplies them many times over because of our faith. At times it may seem like faith is more important to your salvation, because your works appear so tiny compared with how far you've come. At other times, it may seem like works are more important to your salvation, because what you've been asked to do seems monumental. This is normal.

There is a balance that you must maintain between faith and works in your life. If you have great faith but can't ever seem to get off your backside to do something about your faith, then you need to focus on works.[1] If you accomplish all sorts of wonderful works, but can't seem to believe that Christ wants to save someone like you, then you need to focus on faith.[2]

In a similar way, if your driving skills are terrible, you would crash the greatest vehicle in the world. On the other hand, if your vehicle is in a sorry state of repair, the best driver in the world would still crash it.

Vehicles aren't the only example of this concept. I could ask which is more vital, blood, or a functioning heart? Which is more important, a brain, or a spinal cord? What do you need to play soccer, a human or a ball? Which is the more important part of electromagnetic radiation, the magnetic field or the electric field? The answer to all these questions is both. When a system needs two parts in order to function, it is rather silly to ask which part is more important. The system fails without both. The same could be said of faith and works.

In the gospel of Jesus Christ, a more appropriate example might be a thousand-mile journey on a bus. You need both faith and works to get on the bus. If you don't trust Christ, as the bus driver, you won't get on the bus.

---

[1] James 2:14-17
[2] Eph. 2:8-9

But even when you trust him, if you don't take the few steps required, you also won't get on the bus.

After you are on the bus, it takes faith and works to stay on the bus. You must obey the rules of the bus, or you risk losing your seat. You must also have faith in the bus driver's skill and knowledge, especially when he takes an unexpected route or starts down a canyon road with hairpin turns.

Both faith and works are vital on our journey to ultimate salvation.

So, what is salvation then? In a general, secular sense, it's different things to different people.

To the man or woman going through bankruptcy, money is salvation. To the rich man or woman whose lifelong pursuit of money is destroying their close relationships, less money may be salvation. More time alone is a godsend if your life is especially busy at the moment. More time alone is one of the worst forms of punishment for a prisoner who just finished a few months of solitary confinement.

People usually agree that salvation, in a religious context, means getting into Heaven, but if you ask them what Heaven means to them, there is no longer any agreement.

I had a seminary teacher who often joked that if there wasn't football in Heaven, he wasn't going. Many people outside the United States might have a similar sentiment but toward association football not American football.

I have a coworker who insists his Heaven will include rivers of beer and lots of pretty women. To most Latter-day Saints this certainly wouldn't be their first idea of Heaven.

If everyone in the world wrote a prioritized list of the top ten items or activities they expect to see in Heaven, you would get all sorts of responses. Some of the lists would read like a who's who of sins: sex, alcohol, drugs, or violence. Other lists would be less graphic but still focused on personal indulgences: favorite foods, money, video games, sports, entertainment, etc.

If we were to separate out all the lists done by little kids, we would probably see different types of answers. I'm sure the top three things my four-year-old daughter wants in Heaven are flowers, rainbows, and sunshine. My six-year-old son had a special relationship with his great-grandma before she died. He once told me that when he gets to Heaven, he's going to find Grandma Tia and thank her for the cowboy boots.

In reality, if you were to sit down and write such a list, it may start out with things like favorite foods or entertainment, but if you truly thought about it, those things would quickly fall aside to make room for more important things, like family members.

Salvation is a little like an amusement park. When I take my family to the local amusement park, everyone is excited, but if you ask each of my kids why they are excited, you will get different answers. My teenagers see the amusement park as a way to get as much adrenaline as possible into their system without actually vomiting. My younger kids are excited to see their favorite princess or movie character. We parents usually just go to see the smiles on our kids' faces and to make memories, even if making that many memories in one day often gives the dad a massive headache.

Expectations about salvation and Heaven may be different for each of us, but what about the actual Heaven? Isn't there just one Heaven that we are all supposed to be happy with . . . especially considering the alternative?

We can answer this question with the following fictional story of the three sultans:

In the thirteenth century, three sultans each lost their sultanates, or kingdoms, and were banished to the wilderness. The three sultans were used to a wealthy and extravagant lifestyle, so the desert was especially harsh on them.

During one particular sandstorm, the sultans found shelter in a cave. To their surprise, they found a jar with a sealed cap. They immediately cut the seal, and a powerful genie appeared.

This particular genie was neither good nor bad, but he was happy enough to be free of the jar that he offered each of the sultans one wish.

The sultans were overjoyed and praised their luck. They had heard many stories of powerful but evil genies that gave curses instead of wishes. They quickly asked for their kingdoms back, remembering to thank the genie for the blessing.

After hearing their wishes, the genie laughed. He told them that he offered them a wish, not a blessing. Granting a wish could be either a blessing or a curse; it depended on what you asked for. He warned the sultans that he had given out many wishes during his time, and almost every wish he granted had turned into unhappiness by the time the person reached their deathbed.

The sultans all confirmed they wanted their kingdoms back. The genie hugged his belly and laughed. He was certain they had all chosen poorly.

The first sultan couldn't stand his wisdom being questioned. He huffed at the genie, saying the imposter who had taken over his kingdom was an evil man who had killed his wife and children in front of his very eyes. If anyone deserved a slow painful death, it was him. He vowed to sweeten his revenge by watching every minute of the imposter's suffering.

The genie stomped with laughter. It was wonderful to be out of the jar to watch the foolish humans again. He told the first sultan that seeking happiness in other people's pain was the quickest way to destroy your own happiness.

The second sultan stepped forward. His kingdom was the richest in the land but was lost to a neighboring kingdom. His wish would certainly bring him lifelong happiness. His wealth had brought him leisure and comfort. He would spend the rest of his days with the finest foods and the largest harem.

The genie collapsed in laughter. Humans will never understand. He told the second sultan that seeking happiness in comfort and leisure can never produce lasting happiness. It only makes you nothing more or less than comfortably unhappy.

The final sultan approached the genie. He admitted that he would probably fail the wager, because he wasn't seeking his own happiness. His kingdom had been a lovely place to live. His people weren't the richest or the strongest, but they were happy. He had lost his kingdom to a famine, and his people were starving. He wanted his kingdom back, so he could bring a happy life to his people again.

The genie's laughter subsided. This was the beginning of a wise ruler. He told the final sultan that, paradoxically, lasting happiness could most often be found in seeking happiness for others, and if wealth and power did not distract you, happiness would fill your deathbed.

We see from this story that happiness is a rare treasure. Most people spend large amounts of time seeking happiness but often have a difficult time recognizing it. When true happiness comes knocking at the door, we often mistake it for misery or too much work.

To make this concept clearer let's go through an exercise. Let's assume the richest man in the world dies today, and in his will, he leaves all his money to you. What would you do? The possibilities may seem endless, but in actuality, the various things you can do with enormous amounts of money can be grouped into three broad categories.

The first category includes any form of settling the score. You probably wouldn't call it revenge, but that's what it would be. Maybe you wouldn't use your money to actively attack that one boss who made your life miserable for all those years, but you would love to see the look on his face when you give a generous amount of cash to a close acquaintance of his and refuse to give a penny to him. Then he would feel some of the same pain he inflicted on you.

Or maybe you would pay a visit to that high school teacher who said you wouldn't amount to anything. You would love to make him eat his words.

The second category of possible things you could do is to start a party that would never end. Maybe this party involves riotous living or maybe it just involves lots of travel and expensive foods. The point is that you would never have to work another day of your life.

The third category involves using your money to help as many people as you can. Pick a global problem and get to work. Sure, you may buy some things for yourself that you never could have afforded before, but your time and energy would be spent in a cause, not in leisure.

Salvation is much like getting billions of dollars, and Heaven is what you do with it. When we talk about the three degrees of Heaven in the restored gospel of Jesus Christ, we are simply describing this concept.[3] Heaven is not a location as much as it is a state of being.

In the restored gospel, the word Heaven usually means the highest degree in Heaven. This is reserved for those who become like God in every sense of the word.

---

[3] See D&C 76

They will spend eternity doing the infinite amount of work required of a god.

In this context—and setting aside the topic of innocent children for the moment—the gospel is highly exclusive in that relatively few will make it to, or want to be in, this degree of Heaven.

In other contexts within the gospel, Heaven means all degrees of Heaven. This includes almost everyone who ever lived on Earth. The infinite atonement of Jesus Christ has the power to save everyone. There is only one group of people it cannot save: those who refuse to be saved. I'm not talking about those who refuse to believe in Christ on this Earth. I'm talking about at the final judgement when God and Christ offer a type of Heaven to each individual. A small class of people will look God in the face and scream, "Not fair!" These people will declare the whole plan of salvation a fraud and refuse to participate. They will eventually get exactly what they want: they will be left to their own devices.

In this context, the gospel is semi-universalist. Almost everyone will be saved.

In yet another context, the gospel is completely universalist, because the atonement of Christ saves everyone from death. All will receive a resurrected body which will never die. The time to refuse this gift was in the pre-Earth life. Everyone who is born on this Earth will ultimately live forever, the old and the young, the saint and the sinner.[4]

Why does the concept of Heaven have to be so complex? Because God is both fair and merciful. You can have a simple and fair system of salvation, but it won't be merciful. You can have a simple and merciful system, but it won't be fair.[5] God has figured out a way to be completely fair while at the same time ensure everyone has as much happiness in Heaven as they are capable of handling.

God's plan of salvation can certainly seem a little complex at times, but we can never say it is unnatural. We see the same concept occurring all the time. When I take my kids to the local amusement park, they each have the tendency to selfishly seek out their own happiness to varying degrees. Sometimes they seem to actively pester their siblings, almost as if they are only happy if their brother or sister is crying. Other times they focus on the rides and attractions *they* want without regard to anyone else's wishes. But every once in a while, I see hope. I see one of my children sacrifice something they really want just to see a smile on someone else's face.

---

[4] See 1 Cor. 15:22 or 2 Ne. 9:22
[5] Alma 42:25-26

One day you will stand before God at the final judgement. He will offer you salvation through the atonement of Jesus Christ, along with a key into Heaven. Will you snatch up the key and rush into your personalized Heaven, complete with everything you've ever hoped for—and sometimes demanded? Or will you return the key to God and say, "Thank you, but before I enter Heaven, can I first help the billions who are still struggling to get to this point?"

For many, the last option doesn't sound much like Heaven; it just sounds like a bunch of work. Well . . . it is. It's the work and glory of a god.[6]

---

[6] Moses 1:39

Chapter 14

Saving Ordinances

My wife and I periodically take our kids hiking. Like most parents, we want our kids to be safe, so we indoctrinate them in all the hiking rules. Like most kids, our children use endless questions and logic to decide how faithfully they need to obey the rules.

Most of the hiking rules we don't really come up with ourselves. They are just a direct result of the nature of hiking. If I ask my daughter to bring water, it's not because I just want to watch her carry a heavy water bottle the whole time. The nature of hiking simply demands that we bring water, especially in our desert climate. Similar things could be said about other natural rules of hiking, such as bringing hats, wearing shoes, following the trail, and not hiking during flash floods.

My children usually have no problem following these sorts of rules. It's the rules and restrictions my wife and I *do* make which my kids sometimes have a hard time following.

One such rule is the dreaded "parent-in-front, parent-in-back" rule. No matter how many questions they ask, and no matter how many times we explain the reasoning behind the rule, a few of my children just don't understand why Mom is always in front and Dad is always in back, or vice versa. We grownups are just so slow, or boring, or smelly, or some other such undesirable.

Of course, the reasoning behind the rule became dreadfully clear the day I was in front and came within inches of stepping on a rattlesnake before I saw, and heard, what it was. I was able to throw out an arm and stop my six-year-old son from stepping directly on the snake.

The "parent-in-front, parent-in-back" rule is a parent-derived rule, while the "bring water" rule is a natural rule. My wife and I, as heads of the household, create and implement the parent-derived rules. We have our reasons behind these rules, but sometimes the reasoning may not be obvious to our children. The reasoning behind natural laws, on the other hand, are usually clear to everyone involved.

We are children of Heavenly Parents and are trying to become like them. In order to be reunited with them, we must follow natural laws and God-derived laws. Up to now, we have mostly discussed natural laws. For example, if we want to become like God, we must overcome sin and death. Sinful mortals are not like God. That is just the nature of what it means to be God.

On top of all the natural laws, our Heavenly Parents, as heads of the heavenly household, can add as many God-derived laws as they see fit. The reasoning behind these laws may not be as obvious as natural laws, but the reasoning is still there. Any of these God-derived laws can be important enough for God to require all of us children to strictly obey them if we ever want to enter Heaven, just as I may strictly require adherence to a parent-derived rule if a child is to accompany us on a hike. Saving ordinances are in this category. God requires us to fulfill a handful of ordinances, or we simply won't be reconciled with God and allowed into Heaven.

Why would God choose to use ordinances or rituals? Why is a ritual so important that God would require one before allowing us into Heaven? The answer is clear once we understand what an ordinance or ritual really means.

All religions have ordinances or rituals of some sort. This is even true of religions such as Buddhism or Confucianism which some people may classify more as a way of life rather than a religion. In fact, most organizations that are completely secular have rituals, from the local school graduation to the Annual Nobel Prize Awards Ceremony.

You might say that ritual isn't really a religious thing, it's more of a human thing. Humans are ritualistic whether we are religious or not. This is true in simple events, like introducing a new acquaintance to your friend, or large events, like weddings.

I found out the importance of ritual first hand in my own engagement to be married. As a stereotypical scientist who, at times, has been classified as socially challenged, the rituals surrounding engagement and marriage were difficult to navigate.

My wife and I were best friends for years before we officially began dating. After a reasonably long courtship of five months—reasonably long by Latter-day Saint standards—my wife and I began to talk of marriage.

The talk soon turned to plans: we picked out and purchased a ring, we selected a date a few months down the road, and we agreed that I should schedule a room at the temple. I assumed all these fixed plans meant we must be engaged, so I began to tell my family.

Well . . . apparently she hadn't told her family yet. I may not be an expert in social interaction, but even I know that it is probably not a good thing for my future mother-in-law to find out about the engagement of her daughter from a random neighbor who is a mutual friend of the two families.

It turns out my wife didn't feel officially engaged until a few rituals were completed. I had to present her with the engagement ring. This was still true even though she was there when I purchased it.

Of course, none of this was logical to me, but if she had to be in possession of the ring before it was all official, I saw no problem with giving it to her.

I wrapped it up in a Hawaiian shirt I had borrowed for an activity and had to return to her that evening.

I'm not sure which is more unbelievable: that I sincerely saw no reason why using a dirty shirt as wrapping paper might turn out badly, or that my wife still eventually married me.

After another social interaction lesson, a process I have become intimately familiar with over the years, it was explained to me that the ritual didn't just involve transfer of possession of the ring, it involved placing one of my knees on the ground, stating a specific set of words in the form of a question, and then waiting for a reply. This was still true even though I already knew the answer. Well . . . I knew the pre-dirty-laundry answer. Luckily for me, my wife has an inhuman amount of mercy within her.

Why do we humans hold to these rituals, even when they may not be strictly necessary from a logical point of view? Because ritual is just another form of communication. A similar question is, why do we humans use language? We simply do.

Humans use language to communicate just like we use ritual to communicate. This is the case even if some of us aren't all that fluent in some of the forms of communication. Yes, my wife and I were essentially engaged before I went through the ritual, but the ritual still communicated something important.

Shopping together, setting dates, and scheduling are the same types of preparation you might make for something completely normal, like a fishing trip, or for something rather dreadful, like transferring prisoners across state lines. The ritual of getting down on one knee and speaking the words someone has looked forward to their whole life signifies that this is not just some convenient arrangement, but something that will last forever. It is a special arrangement, and it should be treated as such.

So why does God use ordinances and ritual? For the same reasons. If he wants to communicate with us humans, he is simply going to have to use the native forms of communication, and if he wants us to treat our relationship with him in a special way that will last forever, ritual is key.

Baptism is the most famous of these rituals or ordinances. It is classified as a saving ordinance, because Christ specified baptism as strictly necessary to enter Heaven.[1] There are other saving ordinances in the restored gospel of Jesus Christ, some of which are administered in temples. Non-saving ordinances also exist, which are ordinances that are a good idea but not strictly required, just as bringing a snack or a field guide on a hike is a good idea but not strictly required.

So, if becoming like God is already an impossible task, why in the world did he go and stack a bunch of other requirements on top of what was already necessary? Isn't that just pouring salt in the wound?

While participating in ordinances and fulfilling the covenants and promises associated with them might seem a little painful or troubling from our limited perspective, they are *saving* ordinances. God implements them to save us. Yes, pouring salt in a wound is painful, but salt is a natural antiseptic. In the ages before modern medicine, it was really one of the best ways to treat wounds.

All religious ordinances share some features—they use symbolism to teach and ceremony or repetition to help us remember what we are covenanting—but each one has a different reason behind why it is strictly

---

[1] John 3:3-5

required to enter Heaven. I don't intend to discuss each ordinance individually and describe why it is a requirement in the Gospel of Jesus Christ. I simply intend to discuss the consequence of God implementing such requirements.

For example, if God says baptism is required to enter the Kingdom of Heaven, what about all the people who die without ever hearing the word baptism or without ever understanding what baptism means. How could God be considered a fair God if he damns all people who were born in non-baptizing cultures? How could he condemn children who didn't get baptized simply because they died ten minutes after birth? The answer is that God created a way for everyone to fulfill all the saving ordinances, even if they lived their whole lives in an uncontacted tribe in the jungles of Peru.[2]

First, most of the saving ordinances are only required for those who have reached the age of accountability.[3] Baptism is for the remission of sins. Little children are innocent and have no sin. The same can be said about little children for all other saving ordinances except one. The sealing ordinance links families together so they can maintain family relationships in Heaven. This

---

[2] 1 Ne. 3:7
[3] See Moro. 8:10, D&C 18:42, and D&C 68:27

ordinance is administered in temples and is required even if you are an innocent child.

So, what can be done for adults who die before receiving all the saving ordinances and little children who died before receiving the sealing ordinance? This is the reason the Gospel of Jesus Christ allows for ordinances to be done on behalf of those who have died.[4] In fact, this is an easy way to decide whether an ordinance is a saving ordinance or a non-saving ordinance. If we do that ordinance on behalf of the dead, then it is a saving ordinance.

The doctrine of ordinances for the dead is the only way we, as a church, can claim exclusive priesthood authority, yet still be semi-universalist. We have been charged with the task of completing all required ordinances for everyone who has ever lived on the Earth. Of course, we start with our ancestors and others for whom we have records. At some point, after all the records on Earth are done, we will need access to some of the records in Heaven to complete the work.

Eventually, everyone who died without the saving ordinances will either accept or reject the ordinances done on their behalf. You might think, "Who in their right mind will reject ordinances of the Gospel of Jesus Christ after

---

[4] See D&C 124:29-31 and 1 Cor. 15:29

they've died and seen the bigger picture?" Probably the same people who spent their whole life rejecting the Light of Christ, that inner voice which subtly encourages us to do better and become better. Death doesn't change who we are.[5] It is just the next stage of development.

The caterpillar who nibbles on some food here and there but spends the majority of his time kicking back and relaxing won't have sufficient calories to become a butterfly. No amount of chrysalis time is going to help. His growth is stunted.

In the same way, no number of ordinances are going to help the person who spent his whole life trying to distract himself from what he knew, deep down, was the real reason for this life. If he didn't want the change that comes with seeking God in life, he won't want the change that is required with those same ordinances in death.

But if ordinances can be accepted after death, why don't we just live our lives as best we can and ignore all ordinances until after death? It only takes an elementary study of each saving ordinance and its associated covenant to learn that God promises us specific blessings for keeping these covenants. The prospect of living life

---

[5] Alma 34:34

with these blessings as opposed to living life without these blessings makes the answer clear.

So, if ordinances are God-derived rules, and God promises specific blessings in return for entering the covenants associated with these ordinances, where does Christ come in the picture? The saving ordinances are what tie us to Christ. In our previous example of the rescue swimmer, the ordinances and covenants are the straps and clips which he uses to secure us, the victim, to himself.

In reality, you don't need any ordinances for Christ to touch your heart and invite you to come unto him. But after completing these ordinances, Christ doesn't just touch your heart, he wraps his arms around you. He doesn't just invite; he lifts you on his shoulders.

Chapter 15

Authorized Religion

Smallpox has killed untold millions throughout the previous ages. If you contracted smallpox, the likelihood that you would die could be higher than thirty percent.

Smallpox is a disease caused by a virus, so if you caught it and survived, your immune system would protect you from catching it again. Historical cultures understood at least the basics of this fact and found ways to protect themselves and their families. Beginning from at least 1500 in China and 1700 in India, the Ottoman Empire, and parts of Africa, people practiced what is now called variolation to protect themselves and their families from the dreaded smallpox.

Variolation was a primitive form of vaccination where a skilled practitioner crushed dried scabs from a previous victim of smallpox, scratched the shoulder of a child or other unprotected individual, and rubbed the powdered scabs into the scratch. If done successfully, the patient would get a mild, localized case of smallpox which still gave them immunity to the full-fledged version of the disease. If done incorrectly, the patient would contract the full disease and potentially infect others, causing an outbreak in their village. Even if variolation was done by an expert, as many as two percent of people undergoing the procedure would still die.

If a village has to choose between losing two percent of their population now or thirty percent of their population in the inevitable outbreak, the choice is clear.

Visitors from England saw variolation practiced in the Ottoman Empire and India in the early 1700s, and brought the process back home. Soon, doctors all over Europe and North America were offering this new salvation from smallpox.

Variolation was sometimes done sloppily and new outbreaks would result. The governments of Europe responded by either regulating the practice or outright banning it.

In 1796, Edward Jenner discovered that implementing a similar process to variolation, but with the scabs of someone with cowpox, still gave protection against smallpox. His method was superior to variolation in every way and rarely resulted in complications or death. This new form was named vaccination, after "vacca", the Latin word for cow.

From 1959 through 1979, a global campaign to rid the world of smallpox using Jenner's vaccination was successful. Particular organizations were set up to regulate the authorized production and administration of the vaccine to ensure safety and potency. Because of this campaign, untold millions of lives have been saved over the last forty years and into the future. Without careful coordination and regulation, this would not have been possible.

Imagine if the global organization to eradicate smallpox allowed local teams to do whatever they wanted. What if there were no specific standards and no authorized local chapters? Isolated areas of Pakistan and Afghanistan were still practicing the same variolation techniques they had been using for hundreds of years. Their supplies of smallpox scabs were confiscated. If not, they could have caused a new outbreak with just one botched case.

It isn't just in the medical field where regulation and proper authorization are required to accomplish large tasks. We see this in a local municipality that would like to bring clean water to its residents and a country that would like to improve its economy. Most people would agree that regulations and authorizations are necessary, even after they have seen instances where regulation has been used for nefarious purposes.

For example, many business owners wish there were fewer regulations imposed by government. Some might even wish there were no governmental regulations at all. Of course, if they were to try to do business without protective regulations such as patents or property rights, they would soon see why regulation is necessary. It should also be clear to them that a form of authorization from the government is vital. Printed money only works by authorization. Doing business without money would be quite difficult.

In fact, for a society to function it must do so under some form of regulation and with a clear authorization, even if it is nothing more than self-regulation and authorization by the collection of individuals involved.

This rule is no different in religious society. If God is to implement any ordinance or ritual for the salvation of mankind, some form of regulation and authorization is necessary. Otherwise, he would not be in control of the message and covenant associated with the ordinance.

When I am out working in the yard on a Saturday morning and my wife is gone teaching her class, my young son often likes to watch me work. Let's say I instruct him to go inside and remind the rest of the kids to clean their rooms before Mom gets back. My son may go inside and yell, "Dad says you have to clean the whole house right now or he is going to cancel your video game time!" This message is harsher than it needs to be, and it doesn't say anything about getting done before Mom gets back, but if the other kids follow that instruction, it may be acceptable enough.

I can't expect a young child to transfer the message perfectly, but at some point, a line is crossed. If he would have said, "Dad says you have to clean the whole house, or you're kicked out of the family!" that clearly needs to be corrected. Especially with my four-year-old daughter, Maren, who is sensitive enough that she might begin to tearfully pack her bags.

The reason everyone, except Maren, wouldn't take a message like that seriously is because my wife and I have a clear system in place with regulations and authorizations. A job chart is on the wall, and everyone knows their assigned duties, which rotate every week. They also know that when Mom or Dad is home, none of the kids are authorized to change the job chart.

If God wants to require certain ordinances, like baptism, to get into Heaven, he has to set up an authorized religion.

But isn't that a bad idea? Doesn't organized religion dominate, oppress, and sometimes even wage war? Yes, religions have done each of these things, but these behaviors are not restricted to religious organizations. Any collection of humans in a society, whether religious, scientific, economic, or cultural, has also engaged in such behaviors.

Organized religion can be messy primarily because human society can be messy. Of course, the fact that God is willing to wade into the muck and grime of humanity in order to clean things up should be no surprise. He is willing to deal with the messiness of your individual life. Why wouldn't he be willing to deal with the messiness of society as well?

The fact that organized religion still struggles to rise above humanity's natural tendencies should also be no surprise. Don't you still struggle to rise above your natural tendencies, even long after allowing God into your life?

So, if God were to use organized religion to shape individuals and societies, would he use just one authorized church or would he work through all religions on Earth? Again, the deceptively simple answer is both.

If God wants to implement ordinances and control the message and covenant of that ordinance, he must have a single authorized religion,[1] but that doesn't mean he ignores everybody else.

If our Heavenly Parents want to save their children, they are going to use every method available to

---

[1] Eph. 4:5

them to do so. They are always willing to reach out to one of their children and invite them to begin a relationship with them. This is true regardless of religious membership, personal beliefs, or current spiritual state.

When my wife and I go out for a date, our two teenagers are authorized to take care of the other kids. This doesn't mean we love our teenagers and hate our other kids. We love all our kids. That is why we put our teenagers in charge with strict instructions about dinner. Everyone gets dinner, even though it may not always be perfect.

God has only one authorized religion on the Earth at a time but also reaches out to us regardless of our religious membership. This is taught in the parable of the leaven, or yeast.[2] Christ compared the Kingdom of God to yeast put into a lump of bread. The yeast was put there to raise the whole loaf. The authorized church of God, like the yeast, has an important job, but in the end, God isn't going to throw away everything but the yeast. He wants the whole loaf.

It is comforting to know that salvation is within reach through the atonement even if we never belong to God's authorized church in this life, but for many people, partaking in official ordinances and entering into

---

[2] Matt. 13:33; Luke 13:20-21

covenants directly with God is the more desirable option. For them, the only remaining question is: "Which church is God's authorized church?" It would be nice if the answer to this question were clear and widely known. Then we wouldn't have to put forth any effort to know.

I used to work as a physics tutor in college. As every tutor knows, the last thing you want to do is just give people the answer for free—partly because you want them to appreciate the answer and partly because if you just give them the answer, no learning occurs. God, as the greatest teacher, isn't just going to tell us which of all the many churches is his officially authorized church without at least some effort on our part.

So, what particular effort is required, and how much effort does it take to get such an answer from God? This is the topic of the next section.

PART THREE

Holy Ghost

Chapter 16

Spiritual Communication

A few months after I got my driver's license, I was driving down a country road near my house when I got an impression that I should make a U-turn. I hesitated only a moment before turning the car around. After about thirty seconds of driving in the opposite direction, I began to feel foolish. I turned the car back around and continued on toward my original destination.

If this were one of those faith-promoting stories you sometimes read, now would be the part where I insert something about passing a car wreck that happened minutes before or crossing paths with someone who needed my help whom I would have missed otherwise.

What actually happened was a big nothing. I arrived at my destination without mishap and finished out a completely normal day. The only reason I remember this experience at all is because it was difficult for me to process. I spent lots of time wondering if some truck would have hit my car, but because I was ninety seconds too late, nothing happened. Deep down, I also wondered if the thought to make a U-turn was just one of those silly little thoughts that flit through my brain all the time.

This was probably the first time I realized that personal revelation or spiritual communication was not always as easy as I was taught in primary class or that I later taught as a missionary to people learning about the church. It was this experience that led me to believe my understanding of spiritual communication had to mature.

When we pray to God, he speaks to our heart and mind through our feelings and thoughts.[1] This is the simplified version of personal revelation we teach to children and new members. Of course, simplified doesn't mean wrong, it just means this understanding may not be sufficient to explain the full breadth of experiences we might have as we strive to communicate with our Heavenly Parents.

So, what is a mature understanding of personal revelation? To answer this, let's look at the following example:

Assume you seriously injure yourself and are transported to a hospital for treatment. Your injury is examined, and a few tests are done. Finally, the doctor

---

[1] D&C 8:2-3

enters the room to explain the course of action. The only problem is the doctor has a thick accent and likes to use lots of confusing examples from his foreign culture to explain things. All this is complicated by the fact that your injury was largely a result of an underlying condition you've never heard of, the explanation of which has more medical jargon than normal words, that is, if he is even using your native language at all.

From the few words you catch, it looks as if the doctor recommends immediate, emergency surgery, but you're not even sure which organ he plans to operate on, except that a gesture indicates it's somewhere in your abdomen.

The question in this situation isn't, "Do you understand everything the doctor explained about your condition or injury?" The question is, "Do you allow him to operate on you?"

Our understanding of personal revelation and spiritual communication with God is mature when we realize it is usually an unclear process, but we are still expected to make choices based on that unclear process.[2]

Sometimes submitting to God can be as terrifying as quadruple bypass surgery. Other times, it can be more like getting an embarrassing mole removed: a little

---

[2] See D&C 98:12 or 2 Ne. 28:30, for example.

unnerving, but such a relief when it's gone. Whether we submit to God or not is entirely based on this relatively unsure process of spiritual communication.

Spiritual communication is something like echolocation. People who have lost their sight but retain their hearing often develop some proficiency in echolocation. The most proficient could easily navigate an obstacle course simply by listening to reflections of sound waves produced by clicks of the tongue or taps of a cane.

All people with their hearing intact can sense very basic echolocation information. As an experiment, find a sidewalk with a tall brick wall running next to it which ends abruptly. Walk down the sidewalk with some loud shoes while closing your eyes. A friend may have to help you, so you don't accidentally step into oncoming traffic or something. As you walk down the sidewalk you should be able to hear the clicks of your steps bounce off the wall until they abruptly change in volume. You can sense the end of the wall without ever opening your eyes.

People with proficiency in echolocation can not only sense location of large objects such as this, but they can also sense the size and shape of objects, as well as some of their basic material properties.

When someone loses their sight, they don't magically become good at echolocation, they just have much more opportunity to practice echolocating.

Similarly, spiritual communication is a completely different kind of communication. We all have the capacity to learn, but some of us simply do not practice much. Although, some events in our life can more or less force us to practice. These events can be just as traumatic and disorienting as sudden blindness, if not more so.

Echolocation is not perfect, but people can still use it to navigate a path. Similarly, spiritual communication is never perfect, but we can still use it to navigate our life.

But isn't God perfect, you might ask? Why can't a perfect being speak to us perfectly, or at least in a way that we can understand clearly? Because personal revelation at its core is spiritual communication between a perfect God and an imperfect child. It takes two to communicate. Two perfect beings can communicate perfectly, but as soon as one of them is imperfect, communication is imperfect.

For example, my native language is English. I am able to speak quite comfortably in English, but actual communication depends on whom I am speaking with. I have spent almost my entire life in the western United States, so if I converse with someone from the east coast, our communication may be a little less than optimal, depending on where the topic leads. If I were to converse with someone from England, some significant misunderstandings may crop up. If I were to converse with someone who learned English as a second language, even more problems would likely arise.

When our Heavenly Parents speak to our hearts and minds, the result is far from perfect. They are fluent in spiritual communication, while we are just learning. In fact, they are far enough above us that a better comparison might be when a mother speaks to her newborn child.

Newborns know essentially nothing of language, but mothers across the world still speak to their infants—usually in complete sentences—even though limited communication happens. For example, when a mother says, "You're so beautiful!" to her baby, the only thing the baby likely understood is love. The mother didn't use the word "love" in the sentence, but that is the underlying message.

It is no coincidence that most people's first experiences communicating with Heavenly Parents is an impression of love. It is one of the easiest concepts for us to understand. As we begin to learn the language of personal revelation, we can begin to handle more complex messages. In some cases, this means spiritual communication gets clearer as we get more experienced. In other cases, it just means we know enough to make bigger mistakes.

A few years ago, I felt a strong impression I should apply for a tenure-track faculty position at my alma mater.

There was no open position, so I spoke with some of my previous professors who confirmed that a position would open up in a few months. I figured that since the Holy Ghost told me about the position before it was public knowledge I must be on the right track. I applied for the position and quickly rose through the stack of applicants. I was one of the two finalists interviewed for the position. It came as a bit of a shock when I didn't get the job. I had assumed the impression to apply meant I would get the job. My problem was that I had piled a bunch of my own assumptions on top of the spiritual communication. As to why I received the impression in the first place, I'm still not sure.

It might be similar to when a young toddler drops a sandwich in the dirt. After he picks up the sandwich, the mom says, "No no, sweetie. Bring that to me." When he obediently brings the sandwich to his mother, she immediately drops it in the trash. The child starts to cry as he struggles to understand why his mom just threw away his lunch, while his mother, on the other hand, is happy to have protected him from the unseen germs in a mouthful of sand.

When God inspires us to do something, we often assume his long-term intentions are clear. Then we are either disappointed when things don't turn out as we expected, or we completely mess up God's intention as we try to force the outcome we expect.

This problem arises because spiritual communication most often comes to us through our thoughts and feelings. It is all too easy for our own thoughts and feelings to cloud any communication from God. When we ask God a question in prayer, often our own strong thoughts and feelings on the topic fool us into getting the exact answer we wanted, regardless of what God was trying to tell us.

To make matters worse, how do we know when a thought or emotion comes from God and not just from our own subconscious? When a random thought encourages us to do good, it could easily be from God, but what about all those neutral thoughts, like my U-turn thought? How many are from God?

I used to deal with this problem by just assuming if God were to give me personal revelation, it would be a relatively strong impression. I began to ignore the mild thoughts and feelings and pay attention to the stronger ones.

This was a bad idea. Luckily one day I decided to follow the slightest of silly little impressions, and through a series of events over the course of a few months, I completely changed someone's life. I possibly even saved their life.

Personal revelation through spiritual communication is, at times, just plain messy and prone to error. If this is the case, why does God prefer to communicate that way? Can't he just speak to us from a cloud, like in the good old days? In actuality, speaking from a cloud doesn't solve the problem.

Let's look at a scriptural example of this. In Alma 20:2-3, Ammon asks the Lord whether he should go up to the king of all the Lamanites to try and convert him. The Lord says, "Thou shalt not go up to the land of Nephi, for behold, the king will seek thy life." The Lord then tells him to go to a different land. Ammon is obediently traveling to this different land in verse eight, when he just so happens to encounter the exact king the Lord told him to avoid. Not surprisingly, the king pulls out his sword and tries to kill Ammon.

The Lord spoke to Ammon in an extremely clear manner, more or less out of a cloud, but if I were in Ammon's shoes, I would be scratching my head. In a stated attempt to protect him from a murderous king, the Lord sent him directly in that king's path.

Looking at the full scripture story, it is clear God had specific plans when he started Ammon down that path, but he certainly didn't make it clear to him beforehand. We can only assume that if God would have told him everything, it would have confused him worse, or otherwise messed up the plan.

The point is that even if God were to come down and speak to you directly, he would still have to explain concepts that would confuse you just as much, if not more. God's view is often completely foreign to you, and he has to explain everything in a terribly inadequate human language. It would be something like the time I tried to explain the basics of Quantum Physics to my eight-year old using only third-grade reading level English. It didn't go so well. He ended up more confused than when we started.

So why should we even try to receive personal revelation or spiritual communication if we can never be sure we understand everything correctly? Because spiritual communication can be unclear and unsure and still be vital to our spiritual health.

The major mistake we usually make is to treat spiritual communication as just an information gathering exercise. If we have a question, God can answer it for us. This is true, but it is only part of the revelatory process.

In our example of the emergency room with the foreign doctor, he wasn't explaining the details about your condition and injury just for your intellectual curiosity. Any information he gave was so you would be willing to submit to surgery.

God doesn't pass out random information whenever we want it, just like you wouldn't expect a heart surgeon to answer your questions about proper toenail care right before your quadruple bypass surgery.

When we ask God for a clear path ahead, he often can only give us enough inspiration for one or two steps. We then have to ask again to see the next step or two.

Why can't he give us all the answers at the beginning? Because we can't handle it or couldn't understand it.

Spiritual communication is much like breathing. Before you start walking down a path, you don't first breathe in enough air for the next one hundred steps. You take a breath for every step or two. Our bodies can't handle too much oxygen at once. We need a constant source to successfully walk down a path. Our spirits are similar. We need constant spiritual communication to successfully travel through life.

At times, spiritual communication may be almost as natural as breathing. You can be guided without too much effort. You may not even notice God guiding your path until you look back at how far you've come.

At other times, God may seem so unreachable that you feel like you're suffocating. If you fast and pray and ask to see the path ahead and don't get anything clear, maybe it's time to take a step into the unknown. If you still don't get any clear guidance, take another step.

What happens if you don't feel like you get any answers from God for years and years? Maybe you're worried too much about the information part of spiritual communication.

My four-year-old daughter Maren is especially timid. If I were to walk with her on a path with rough terrain and loose stepping stones, she would gingerly take each step. She would probably even ask me if every stone were loose before stepping on it. I cannot analyze and discuss every step she takes. If I did that, she would miss the whole point of walking down the path. The easiest way to proceed is for me to take her hand and say, "You're doing great. Keep going."

We often think the primary purpose of spiritual communication is for God to pass information to us, but if God were to give us all the information we ever wanted about every single step in life, we would miss the whole point about walking through life. When you ask for answers about something legitimately important to you, sometimes God just takes your hand and says, "You're doing great. Keep going."

Chapter 17

Unanswered Questions

"Why is the sky blue, Daddy?" my young daughter asked while coloring a picture.

"Rayleigh scattering," I said from behind my book.

After a few failed attempts to say Rayleigh, she simply said, "What's that?"

"Rayleigh scattering is when light travels through a transmissive material, such as the Earth's atmosphere, and a portion of that light is scattered by particles much smaller than the wavelength of the light." I glanced in her direction. "Why do you ask?"

"I need to know which crayon to use, blue or sky blue."

"Oh . . . either one will work."

Little kids love asking questions. Why is the sky blue? How does Santa get down the chimney? How do hummingbirds fly like that? Where do babies come from? Why did Grandma have to die?

We as parents try to answer as best we can, but sometimes the answer is too complex for them to understand. Other times, they could understand just fine, but giving them the answer before they are ready may be a bad idea. Quite often, there is simply no clear answer.

It is interesting to see what children do when they encounter these unanswered questions. Depending on their personality, some of my children are never satisfied with an unanswered question. No matter how many answers I give them, or how many times I say, "I don't know," they will keep asking and asking the same question until they feel like they understand, even if that understanding is faulty.

Some of my other children seem to be especially trusting. If I give an answer that sounds like I know what I'm talking about, they trust me completely, even if they have no concept of half the words I use.

I'm not saying one or the other approach is better. Sometimes relentless questioning is necessary for progression, and other times absolute trust is necessary for progression. Most times, a healthy balance between the two is optimal.

For example, when we go on a family hike, one child can cause problems if he refuses to participate until all his questions were answered about shoes, hats, the UPF-50 designation, GPS devices, GPS satellites, trail markers, mountain lion feeding habits, rattlesnake venom toxicity, location and availability of anti-venom, earthquake likelihood tables, and floodplain maps. In this case, excessive questioning halts progress. On the other hand, there have been times when I trusted my GPS too much and have gotten lost as a result. In some instances, people have died or received serious injury because they trusted the authority of their GPS device unquestioningly.

Unanswered questions are not just for children. We all face unanswered questions in life. Luckily, the objective of this life is not to simply answer as many questions as we can. Heaven isn't God giving a medal to the person who collected the most answers or the most intelligence in life. The objective of this life is to see what we do when we don't have all the answers. That is why this life is a test of faith. When we don't have answers, we have to trust. That is the only option left.

Some people try to evade unanswered questions by avoiding religion altogether. Contrary to popular belief, unanswered questions aren't just reserved for theology or philosophy. They pervade all areas of life and all professions.

Unanswered questions in physics is what caused my so-called crisis of science in the first place. Yes, I knew there were unanswered questions in physics before I started my degree. To some extent, active areas of research are the things that made physics so appealing to me. What I wasn't prepared for were the overwhelming number of unanswered questions, even in relatively mundane topics, such as gravity or electricity.

Whenever an atheist says, "If God were more like gravity, I would believe again," I can't help but think they understand neither God nor gravity. What I believe they are trying to say is gravity is familiar while God is unfamiliar. What I believe they don't realize is just because they are familiar with the effects of gravity doesn't mean they are familiar with gravity itself. We have had three or four different ideas of gravity over the last three or four hundred years, and it is painfully obvious that our current idea of gravity is incomplete in the best case and plain wrong in the worst case. This is readily apparent from the fundamental incompatibility between classical dynamics and quantum mechanics, as seen in the fight between General Relativity and Quantum Gravity.

I don't intend to argue that God and religion deserve a second chance because gravity still has unanswered questions. I merely intend to point out that you can trust in something regardless of whether you completely understand it. Anyone who has studied quantum physics at any level has first-hand experience with this concept. Unanswered questions have less to do with how true something is and more to do with measuring how much trust you place in that something.

For example, if you were to open your purse or wallet and find you were missing fifty dollars, what would you do? Where the money went is the unanswered question. Would you immediately suspect a family member? That is a measure of your trust in family. Would you suspect that you misplaced it or miscounted it? That is a measure of trust in your own memory or abilities.

When we first moved to our little town ten years ago, our first Sunday was a Stake Conference, which involved every Latter-day Saint in the whole town. After the meeting, we returned to the parking lot, and as we started the car, we saw the gas gauge was almost completely empty even though it was full before the meeting. We were upset that in such a small town, someone would sneak into a church parking lot and siphon off the gas from our tank. It didn't even cross our minds that it might have been a member of the church who did it. This was a measure of our trust in the fellow members of our church. What resulted from this experience was that we had very little trust in the town for all of twenty-four hours, until the next day when our car showed a full tank again. That is how we discovered our faulty gas gauge. Apparently, we trusted our relatively old car more than we trusted the people in our town. Now that we have lived here for more than ten years and have become familiar with the people, we have much more trust in our community.

In this example, the unanswered question didn't really help us find out the truth, it just helped us recognize where our trust was strongest. In this case, unfamiliarity with the town meant lack of trust. This can be true in a more general sense as well. Where we place our trust can be primarily affected by where we place our time. If we spend all our free time doing anything and everything except religious activities, then we will constantly struggle to place our trust in religion as opposed to those other things. Where we place our trust can also be a matter of *how* we engage our time. If we view religion as primarily a social club, or a series of service opportunities, then our engagement with our religion can be superficial.

So, when we come across an unanswered question in religion, what do we do? Many of us turn to science, history, or popular opinion to answer the question. When this happens, it just shows us that we trust those other institutions more than religion. This same effect can be seen in science as well. When people come across unanswered questions in science, such as odd-looking pictures of the surface of Mars, they sometimes turn to popular online theories about aliens instead of the less

Hollywoodesque, and more mundane, explanations put forth by planetary scientists.

I'm not trying to argue we should ignore unanswered questions in religion. These questions can point out serious flaws in our worldview. What I *am* arguing is that we as humans are uncomfortable when confronted with unanswered and unanswerable questions. We then get it in our heads that the true worldview must be the one with the least number of unanswered questions. If that were the case, then my four-year old daughter would be justified in believing the sky is blue because someone splashed too much blue paint. From her perspective, that has far fewer unanswered questions than this thing called Rayleigh scattering.

All too often, when we struggle to trust in God it isn't because of the long list of unanswered questions we could hand him, it's because we don't know how to deal with even one unanswered question.

Chapter 18

Knowing the Church is True

I distinctly remember the exact moment, at a young age, when I learned to whistle. I had been sitting under the dining table for what seemed like hours blowing air through my lips with every combination of lip and mouth position I could imagine. Finally, the tiniest bit of sound came out. I spent the rest of the day giving a barely audible, one-note recital to everyone in my family many times over.

I felt like this was the biggest accomplishment of my entire life. My brothers probably dismissed my meager efforts, but I remember my mom and dad listening attentively and giving me far more praise than I deserved.

My oldest son was also fascinated with whistling at a young age. He often begged me to teach him. I did the best I could, but it was difficult to describe much more than the requirement to make a hole with your lips and blow air through it. He tried this and failed.

"You lied!" He said. "Tell me the secret!"

"There is no secret," I replied. "Just try different sizes of holes and different airspeeds while paying attention to what the inside of your mouth is doing, because that seems to be important as well."

He looked at me skeptically, but continued practicing for multiple weeks until he could also give the barely audible, one-note recitals.

So why was his first reaction to my lesson to accuse me of lying or withholding truth? Because we as humans have a hard time recognizing the difference between truth and true. The concepts overlap enough that we can often get away with assuming they are the same thing, but the difference is subtle and sometimes vitally important.

Truth is fundamental; it doesn't change. True is when something points to that underlying truth, or when you bring something into alignment with that truth.

In the case of whistling, I'm sure there is an acoustics scientist somewhere who has studied whistling in great detail. I'm sure she has examined the effects of tongue placement and mouth shape on tone, as well as the specific shape and size of the hole required for each specific note. With that information you could describe whistling with a series of mathematical equations. This effort is an attempt to uncover truth.

The lesson on whistling I gave to my son didn't include rigorous descriptions of acoustics. I didn't pull out the trusty chalkboard for any equations. But even though my lesson didn't include all this truth, it was still true. It was true in the sense that it was aligned with the underlying truth and set him on the path to discover that truth.

The difference between truth and true may be clearer in the house building occupation. When building a house, the fundamental truth is the relationship between gravity and the walls and roof. Other truths are weather, earthquakes, electricity, aesthetics, etc., and their relationship to the structure. The job of the architects and engineers is to include these truths in the house plan. The builder's job is to make the house true to these plans using rulers, squares, levels, etc.

A house can be built true while it may not be obvious to the owner where and how the truths were applied in the construction.

Similarly, a church can be true to the underlying truths of the gospel while it may not be clearly obvious how those truths are captured. A religion can be true, and a person may still succeed or fail while they try to gain an intuitive understanding of the truths of eternity.

Fundamental truth makes perfect sense after you have gone through a true process to gain an intuitive understanding of that truth. When Eliza R. Snow discussed the doctrine of Heavenly Parents, she relied on this fact. "In the heav'ns are parents single? No, the thought makes reason stare! Truth is reason; truth eternal Tells me I've a mother there."[1] She could have quoted scripture or Joseph Smith to back up her claim to a Mother in Heaven, but instead, she relied on the statement "Truth is reason." After we have done the legwork, truth is completely reasonable, but this may not necessarily be the case if we have bypassed the true lesson and aren't in alignment yet.

In the Church of Jesus Christ of Latter-day Saints, we take very seriously the charge to find out for ourselves if the church is true. We ask every potential convert and child of established members to pray to God to know for themselves if the church is true.

How does God answer? Through the Holy Ghost. I tended to be fairly analytical as a young child, so this method was often frustrating to me. I still remember when I finished the Book of Mormon for the first time and prayed to find out if that book and the church were true.

---

[1] Snow, Eliza R. "My Father in Heaven." *Times and Seasons*. Vol 5, pg. 1039. Nov. 15, 1845.

After my prayer, I mostly just remember not being sure if I got an answer or not. I didn't have a negative response to my prayer, I just wasn't sure if the prayer really did anything. Like many young Latter-day Saints, I was probably expecting some overwhelming spiritual experience that left no question in my mind. I wanted one experience I could forever point to when someone asked me how I gained a testimony. What I got was the tiniest grain of something which might have been what testimonies are made of. When I combined this grain with all the other particles received over a lifetime, it turned into a rather large mound of fertile soil in which a testimony could grow.

At the time, I assumed finding out if the church is true would be a simple yes or no question. I didn't quite understand that the point of something being true is to align us with an underlying truth. This is not really a question you answer but more of a process, like learning how to whistle or building a house. After I have built a house, I can confidently state the house plans were true to the truths found in gravity and weather, but the house was really the point of it all, not just that statement.

In the scriptures, Alma compares the process of knowing if his sermon is true to the process of growing a tree from a seed.[2] A careful reading shows that Alma is comparing the unsure nature of faith to the process of knowing if his sermon is true. Finding out if the scriptures are true or the church is true takes faith, patience, and diligence, and will often feel like a completely unsure process. You must apply the words in your life long enough to see the fruit, which will then finally give you some measure of surety. I can know a seed is a good seed, but ultimately the fruit is the point.

Trying to find out if the church is true or if the Book of Mormon is true scripture is much like going on a diet. A dietician can tell us all sorts of truths about healthy food and its effect on the human body, but if we want to be healthier, we need to put that advice into practice.

It would do me no good if I took the healthy food to a chemistry lab and calculated the total nutritional content, the lower values of fats and sugars, decided for myself whether the food is in fact healthy or not, and then never ate it. In a similar way, you can logically analyze the scriptures, you can compare doctrines, you can decide whether the church fits with your worldview or not, but if you never follow its precepts, you're not going to really know if it is true. And even if you knew, it wouldn't do you much good. Its lessons must be folded into your life.

---

[2] Alma 32:26-43

Another way to fail my diet would be to eat one healthy meal, jiggle my belly, say, "Well, that didn't seem to do much," and then quit.

You can't pray once or twice, go to church for a few weeks or months, and then quit because church didn't seem to do much for you. Yes, praying once or going to church once may give you the idea that religion is a good thing for you, but actually finding out if the church is true takes much longer than that. Yes, I may feel healthier after one meal, but if I really want to see if the diet is good, I need to stick with it.

What about all those people who have read scriptures, prayed, and attended church for years but still don't feel like they know the church is true? The reason is similar to the reason why there are people who have followed diets on and off for years and still aren't where they want to be.

One reason is sometimes people haven't really been following the diet all that well. We humans are good at convincing ourselves that we are following the rules when we are only sort of following them. The same goes for religion. Sometimes we think we're internalizing the truths of the gospel as we read, pray, and attend church, but we're only going through the process in a mediocre or superficial manner. If this is the case, we shouldn't be surprised when we get only a mediocre or superficial testimony.

Another reason is that sometimes people are too hard on themselves when it comes to dieting. They have been faithfully following their diet for years, but progress is too slow, or they still aren't as perfect as everyone else around them seems to be. In church, it is all too easy to put ourselves in a similar situation whenever Brother So-and-so pounds the pulpit with his certainty, and you can't help but feel a little singed by the fire of his testimony. We all create in our minds an ideal of what a testimony of the church should be, and too many people just give up after not reaching that ideal without ever realizing how far they've come.

Ultimately, spirituality isn't a competition. Yes, you may still be a little spiritually flabby, but that's fine. In the gospel, unlike in dieting, we have the atonement. It's not how long we've been on the path that counts. It's not how far we've come that is important. The only thing that counts is that we are still on the path trying to move forward, and if we've fallen off the path, that we're scraping and scrambling back toward it as best we can.

So, what about all the people across the world who do not follow the theology of the restored gospel of Jesus Christ and feel like they have an answer from God that their church is true and ours isn't? If the Church of Jesus

Christ of Latter-day Saints is the only true church, wouldn't God only give spiritual guidance toward that church? Hopefully the answer to this question is clear by now.

Yes, we unequivocally claim to be the only true church[3] with sole authorization by God to officiate in his ordinances.[4] Of course, this doesn't mean other churches have a complete lack of truth.

In our house analogy, a proper house must take into account the truths dictated by gravity. If a house cannot stand under gravity, then it isn't a true house, but this isn't the only truth people care about when looking for a house. A house that stands up under gravity but doesn't protect you from the weather is not very useful either. A house that doesn't follow the truths captured in earthquake codes may be perfectly adequate until an earthquake hits. A house can be built true to some truths, but built with complete disregard to other truths.

When we claim to be the only true church, we are claiming to be true to *all* essential truths of the gospel of Jesus Christ. We accept that other churches are true to some fundamental truths, but not all. When you hear the

---

[3] D&C 1:30
[4] D&C 13

terms, "fullness of the gospel" or, "fullness of truth," this is the concept people are usually trying to get at.[5]

Let's attempt to look at this whole situation from God's perspective using this same house analogy. Say you want to help a homeless person find shelter on a dangerously cold night. You wouldn't ask the homeless shelter if they were up to date on the latest earthquake codes. The main thing you would be concerned about is if the person can be sheltered from the weather. You could worry later about getting them on their feet again and into a better housing situation. Even then, their first apartment may not be the most desirable or up to date.

Yes, God has an ideal for you, but when you are in the middle of the storms of life, his first priority is to get you some basic shelter. This can be done in most religions. As you get on your spiritual feet again, he can help you take the next step. This can also be done in most religions.

God inspires people to go to religion in general, because most religions can start a person's spiritual journey. If a person feels like God has shown them their church is true, it is because most churches are true to at least some fundamental truths, and the Holy Ghost testifies of all truth, no matter where it is located.

---

[5] See JS-H 1:34 or 1 Ne. 13:24-29

So why doesn't everyone who is sincerely seeking God and his truth ultimately end up in God's true church? Because, like so many other plans God has for us, this life is only part of our spiritual journey. Much of our spiritual journey is going to take place in the next life.

Does having all the essential truths of the gospel mean Latter-day Saints are better than people from other religions? Of course not. In this example, we all start out homeless. Both church members and non-members are trying to find basic shelter from the storms of life. In the bigger picture, none of us are going to make it too far on our spiritual path before death. There will be much spiritual progression that simply doesn't happen until the next life, both for the member and non-member. As we have discussed multiple times, having the most accurate idea of God or having the most truth is not the primary objective of this life. Complete change is the objective.

Ultimately, knowing the church is true doesn't mean we can sit down and write a list of truths on a piece of paper. Even if we could, we would be missing the whole point of the process. We know the church is true when we look inside ourselves and see the truths of the gospel folded into our soul. We know the church is true when we recognize that we captured these truths somewhere along the path which the church marked for us. The details of exactly which truths were encapsulated in the lessons you got at church aren't as important as the slow, lifelong process of embracing those truths and letting them feed your soul.

When you first recognize the truths soaking into your life, it can be as exciting as my first success with whistling. Years later, you may look back and get frustrated because your testimony seems to have not grown much beyond a barely audible, one-note recital—especially when others around you seem like they've been whistling Dixie their whole life. Luckily, our meager efforts aren't ultimately judged by the self-proclaimed experts all around us but by our Heavenly Parents. And they are ready to give us far more than we deserve.

Chapter 19

We Thank Thee, O God, For a Prophet

The Church of Jesus Christ of Latter-day Saints claims to be the only true church on the face of the Earth, because it has a fullness of the truths of the gospel and is the only authorized church of God. Students of the theology of the restored gospel of Jesus Christ will recognize here only two of the three commonly described supporting pillars of that truth claim. The third is modern prophets or continuing revelation, sometimes described, perhaps more correctly, as a special witness of Jesus Christ.[1]

So, what exactly is a prophet? In a secular sense it just means someone who can tell the future. I can be a prophet for the stock market if I can predict future

---

[1] Oaks, Dallin H. "The Only True and Living Church." Address delivered on June 25, 2010, at a seminar for new mission presidents. ChurchOfJesusChrist.org.

recessions. Of course, science or math-based predictions would not be considered prophecy, except in a derogatory sense. If someone disagreed with the math behind my predictions, they would accuse me of prophesying instead of proper analyzing.

In a religious sense, there can sometimes be a little more confusion on what a prophet does. Some religious people still assume the role of a prophet is restricted to foretelling the future. You see this when a non-member discovers that we claim to have modern prophets and the first thing they ask is, "What has he predicted lately that came true? Then I'll know if he is a real prophet."

Prophets don't predict the future; they warn us about the future. Prophets won't tell us who will win the World Cup, but they will warn us about the future course of our present actions. Yes, prophecy often contains information about the future, but that information is secondary to the real focus of the prophecy: to turn us toward God.

This is an especially difficult concept for literal thinkers or fundamentalists who take every word of a prophecy or scripture absolutely literally. When people stake everything they own on a minutely literal interpretation of a prophecy or scripture, or even worse, on someone else's interpretation, they are misusing that prophecy or scripture.

For example, where I grew up, every winter involved snow and ice. Anyone who has walked down an icy path knows the dangers of ice, especially when it is mostly invisible. My father always taught us boys that it was our responsibility to offer an arm to our date on an icy path, even if it was dreadfully embarrassing to us nerdy kids. This was especially important if our date had those terrible dress shoes they make for women with absolutely no traction. I'm almost certain that some girls would wear shoes with the worst traction on winter nights precisely so they could make me uncomfortable by holding onto my arm all the time.

As a teenager, if I were to pick up may date on an icy winter night and say, "There are three icy patches on the path, a little one and two big ones," I wouldn't tell her this because I want her to go measure the ice and determine if I am correct. I wouldn't tell her so she would be fascinated by the number or size or slipperiness of the ice. I would tell her so she would grab onto my arm and be safe. If I would have just said, "Grab onto my arm, if you will, please," she may have questioned my motives. The mention of ice gives context as to the seriousness of the situation.

When prophets prophesy, they don't often give details or timelines, and when they do, they are only there to give context to the seriousness of our situation. True prophecy and scripture have always existed primarily to turn us toward God. If they warn us about a future event, it shouldn't be our primary objective to use that information to reliably foretell the future.

Why? Because often these warnings are general and difficult to trace clearly into the future or backward into the past. Recently, modern prophets have warned society "that the disintegration of the family will bring upon individuals, communities, and nations the calamities foretold by ancient and modern prophets."[2] This prophecy is in general terms, and people will disagree as to which modern calamity may be due to what past disintegration of the family. It would be difficult to clearly predict the future based on this particular prophecy until long after much disintegration and calamity.

It would be nice if prophecy were always clearer and gave detailed specifics. The trouble is, when we receive absolutely clear prophecy, we usually still can't use it to predict the future. When Jonah prophesied to Nineveh that the city would be destroyed within forty days unless they repented,[3] it would have been a bad idea

---

[2] "The Family: A Proclamation to the World." The Church of Jesus Christ of Latter-Day Saints. 1995, para. 8.
[3] Jonah 3:3-4

to wait forty days and see if the prophecy came true before deciding to repent.

This is another reason why prophecy is misused if it is used primarily to foretell the future. Prophecy is almost always explicitly conditional based on the repentance level of the people to which the prophecy was given, and when it isn't explicit, it is usually implicit. Because repentance levels and the collective heart of the people are difficult to put into equations or logical formulations, getting in the business of foretelling the future based on prophecy or scripture is generally a bad idea. When the original conditions of a prophecy change, God will likely give a new prophecy to his prophet.

When I tell my son to study a few chapters in his textbook or he will get a bad grade on his math test next week, that is a specific warning. If he were to wait to study until 1:00 AM the night before the big test, my warning would change. I would tell him to forget studying and focus on a good night's sleep. That doesn't mean my previous advice was bad; it just means the conditions have changed.

Yes, a prophet can prophesy. Unfortunately, our first instinct is not to heed the warning but to use the prophecy in a futile attempt to decide when to sell a house or when to buy stocks.

We get ourselves into trouble when we think a prophet's sole role is to foretell the future through prophecy. It's better to think of a prophet as an inspired teacher. He has some access to God or insight into his gospel, and then he teaches others the lessons gleaned from this access or insight. This sounds relatively broad. With this definition, all sorts of teachers, men and women, could be considered prophets.

This is exactly what Moses is speaking about when he says, "would God that all the Lord's people were prophets, and that the Lord would put his spirit upon them!"[4]

Notice the inclusion of the spirit or Holy Ghost in Moses's statement. A teacher is not an inspired teacher until they get the Holy Ghost. A prophet isn't an inspired teacher without the Holy Ghost. Naturally, the Holy Ghost is vital for the learner as well as the teacher.[5] This explains why one person can listen to a sermon or read a scripture and be edified while another person can listen to the same sermon or read the same scripture and be bored to tears.[6]

Even though this concept is an important part of a prophet's role, when we talk about prophets in the

---

[4] Num. 11:29
[5] D&C 50:17-22
[6] D&C 33:16

restored gospel, we usually don't just mean a person with the spirit or an inspired teacher. We mean something much more than that. Prophets, in the fullest sense of the word, are something like ambassadors from God.

A governmental ambassador often has a long list of skills. They are often talented managers, have charismatic personalities, and are expert negotiators, but those skills aren't what make ambassadors important. Ambassadors are important because they are authorized to speak for the head of their government. Presidents, prime ministers, or monarchs simply can't dictate every tiny detail of every foreign policy for every single country. When an ambassador speaks in their official position to a foreign government, their word is as binding as if the president or queen had spoken. In practice, this puts tremendous pressure on the ambassador to make sure their official acts are in line with their home government.

A prophet is an ambassador from God in a similar way. God chooses an individual to be his representative to a people or nation. When a prophet speaks, his word is as binding as if God himself had spoken.

Does this mean when the prophet says, "Please pass the salt," it's God's will that you pass the salt? Of course not. A prophet has to speak in his official capacity as prophet for it to count.

Does this mean a prophet will never make a mistake when acting in his official capacity? No. This is an imperfect process, and mistakes are made. Prophets are far from infallible.[7]

So, if a prophet can make mistakes—even big ones—how do we reconcile this with Wilford Woodruff, when he said, "The Lord will never permit me or any other man who stands as President of this Church to lead you astray. It is not in the programme. It is not in the mind of God. If I were to attempt that, the Lord would remove me out of my place . . ."[8] How can a prophet never lead the church astray yet still make big mistakes? The answer lies in the word "astray".

If the church were like a train on a railroad track, then a single wrong direction on any junction will lead the church astray. If the church were like a canoe on a lake, then there is a fair amount of leeway in the pointing direction before the church would be considered astray. And even if mistakes are made for a while, it isn't too much trouble for God to correct the course of the canoe later.

Either of these examples could represent the situation of the church but with drastically different room

---

[7] See, for example, Nu. 20:7-12, Jonah 1:1-3, or Jonah 4
[8] D&C OD 1

for error. Which example is closer to the truth? We don't really know. God is the one who knows. If you think about it, this makes perfect sense. God is the only one equipped with the information to decide whether the Church of Jesus Christ is going astray. And he is perfectly capable of correcting its course.[9] With our limited perspective, we sometimes might think the church is out of line when in fact it is within the tolerances God has set forth.

As an example of this concept, compare the church to an airplane that is coming in for a landing under a heavy crosswind. The pointing angle of the aircraft under such conditions is usually quite different from the angle of the landing strip. A passenger might look and see that the plane is way out of alignment and panic. In reality, the airplane must be misaligned in these conditions until the very last correction right before touchdown.

None of us would presume to go into the cockpit of an aircraft as it is landing during a heavy storm and try to tell the pilot what to do, but we sometimes get the urge to do exactly that to God's prophet.

So where is the balance? Prophets make mistakes on the one hand, yet they are the only ones authorized to dictate the direction of the church on the other hand. How do we deal with this seemingly contradictory situation? If

---

[9] See 2 Sam. 6:6-7

we second guess everything a prophet ever says and wait until we get a direct spiritual communication from God confirming his counsel, there isn't much point to having a prophet in the first place. If we blindly follow everything the prophet says without thinking for ourselves, we never take the opportunity to learn and grow. This is another one of those things for which there is no easy answer. We must put forth the time and effort to find that balance in our personal lives. We should take the prophet's counsel extremely seriously, with a healthy dose of spiritual confirmation when needed.

Why do we need to take the counsel of modern prophets so seriously? Receiving advice and warnings from someone who has direct and continuing access to God is profoundly important. Surprisingly, non-members often more easily recognize this importance before some members. Maybe many of us have become complacent about prophets or take them for granted. It could also be because some Latter-day Saints may inadvertently downplay the direct connection between God and his prophet. Without realizing it, they may focus on a prophet's managerial skills or speaking skills and forget his most important characteristic: God speaking directly to him and asking him to relay a message to us.

So how does this work exactly? When I was a child, I assumed the First Presidency and Quorum of the Twelve

Apostles, the fifteen men we believe are prophets, were given some heavenly earpiece like the type security guards wear, only this earpiece was a direct connection to God. I also figured Christ sat in a sixteenth chair in all their meetings. When I grew up, I was tempted to move to the opposite extreme that the prophets get plain old inspiration or promptings just like the rest of us, with disappointed emphasis on the word "just."

I don't claim to have inside information on the exact nature of the interaction between God and his modern prophets, nor will I speculate. Instead, I will ask, "Does it matter?"

If the ambassador to the United States from Great Britain were to receive a personal phone call from the queen instructing him on a tricky political matter, would he be upset that he only got a phone call instead of a video conference call? Would the embassy staff feel justified in ignoring the queen's advice because it was *just* a phone call instead of a personal audience? If the ambassador had received only an email or text message from the queen, would that information be less important than a phone call?

A personal audience with the queen of England would be spectacular, even life-changing, but an ambassador's authority doesn't rest on how many personal audiences he has had or what method the queen—or in reality, the prime minister or foreign secretary—uses to converse with him. He has the authority to act in the name of Her Majesty's Government even if he is acting based on personal judgement without any specific direction. The British Government would respect his actions even if mistakes are made periodically. That is what it means to be an ambassador.

Modern prophets are important, not because of how many times they have seen God or heard his voice, but because they are authorized by God. The prophet has sole authority as to how and when priesthood ordinances are done. He can speak for God to anyone anywhere. If he makes mistakes, large and small, God doesn't immediately pull out the lightning bolts. He works with him, just like God continues to work with us in spite of our mistakes, large and small.

We sometimes call modern prophets special witnesses of Jesus Christ. Sometimes this is literal, because they have seen and talked with Christ. But far more importantly, regardless of whether they have actually seen Christ or not, they know Christ. They know his gospel. They know what to do to help people become more like him. They have been asked to be his representatives to the world. They are special witness of Jesus Christ, because their job is to help others come to know him.

This concept is what Moses was getting at when he wished everyone were prophets. In a similar but less official way, our job is to help others come unto Christ. For many of us, this first means we need to get to know Christ. This has relatively little to do with whether you've seen Christ's face in a vision. All sorts of people saw Christ's face when he was alive, but relatively few actually knew Christ. To come to know Christ, we must come to know his message and then follow him. Do what he asks us to do.

At the final judgement, all of us will see the face of Christ. The ultimate question at that point will not be whether you've seen his face before in some dramatic spiritual manifestation, but if others have seen his face through yours.[10]

---

[10] See Alma 5:19, Moro. 7:46-48, and 1 Jn. 3:1-3

Chapter 20

Baptism of Fire

I grew up in a house filled to overflowing with boys. In an attempt to lessen the chaos, my parents were constantly trying to get us to do chores, which involved cleaning, cooking, laundry, and the periodic brood of chickens. Naturally, we boys were constantly trying to avoid the above-mentioned chores.

One day, my mother started yet another system to encourage us to work. She walked in and announced to us that she had hidden candy in each of the rooms which we were assigned to clean. She sat us down for a quick lesson on how in life there are natural rewards that come to those who learn how to work hard. We nodded happily at the lesson and rushed to our assigned rooms. Mine was the bathroom.

I quickly saw the large stick of old-fashioned taffy partially concealed under a rug. I snatched it up, shoved the towels and toothbrushes to the corners of the room to make it look like I had cleaned, and then tore off the wrapper.

Needless to say, the new system of natural rewards didn't last the hour.

All parents reward and punish their children. My wife and I have tried our fair share of systems in an attempt to get our children to do their household jobs. My boys especially love the "clean for nineteen play for five" system. It all started one day when the boys had no desire to clean; they just kept begging to play video games—a relatively common day. I finally gave up being the taskmaster and told them if they cleaned for twenty minutes, they could play for five minutes. They could then alternate twenty and five as many times as they wanted, as long as they set a timer and kept track carefully. They haggled me down to nineteen minutes of cleaning, because nineteen is so much shorter than twenty, at least to a child's mind.

The first few times it seemed to work. They cleaned and played and cleaned and played. I used the system more often over the next few weeks, figuring I had stumbled upon parental genius, but getting children to do their chores is like a familial arms race. Every new system, no matter how foolproof, is eventually exploited. My kids began to focus entirely on their paused game. They discovered that they could spend the nineteen-minute timer mostly staying out of their parents' sight if they periodically walked through the living room with a random object in their hand and an intent look on their face. I'm almost certain that one time we went through three cycles of "cleaning" without a single toy being put away, just lots of intent walking.

Why do parents go to great lengths setting up systems of rewards and punishments to get their children to clean their rooms? Contrary to what my children may believe, we don't just enjoy holding over their heads the threat of punishment or promise of future reward. The punishment or reward is not the focus of the system. They are tools we use to teach them. The clean room isn't even the focus—I could clean my kids' rooms in a fraction of the time. We are trying to teach them to work hard, to be responsible, and to sacrifice for the family. If they want to be a successful parent one day, these are lessons they will have to learn.

So, what sort of punishments and rewards does God set up for us? There are all sorts of systems. I don't intend to talk much about the punishments. This world is full enough with sorrow and heartache that often the only punishment God needs to give is exactly what we demand of him—to leave us alone. When left to our own devices, we tend to punish ourselves.

I'm not trying to say God never actively punishes people, I just suspect it happens less often than we think. Why actively punish wicked people when the natural consequences of wickedness tend to be punishment enough?[1]

The natural consequences of our good actions can be a reward God uses as well. Unfortunately, the relatively long timelines for natural consequences, both good and bad, don't lend themselves well for immediate feedback. Without this feedback, we are the equivalent of little kids who don't stick with difficult tasks for long. To mitigate this effect, God uses the Holy Ghost.

The Holy Ghost is one of the major ways God rewards us. We read in the scriptures that the fruits of the spirit are "Love, joy, peace," and a host of other good things.[2] Another category of rewards the Holy Ghost provides are the gifts of the spirit.[3]

For most of our lives these fruits and gifts of the spirit will be our primary way to recognize if the path we are on is the one God wants us to be following. At a fundamental level, if we feel like the spirit is with us, manifested by at least some of these fruits or gifts, then we

---

[1] Alma 41:10
[2] Gal. 5:22-23
[3] See D&C 46:10-26, Moro. 10:8-18, or 1 Cor. 12:8-11

are following God's path for us,[4] at least at some acceptable level.

To recognize whether we have the spirit or not isn't necessarily as easy as it sounds. The devil has a counterfeit to each of these fruits or gifts. Do we really feel love for those around us, or do we just like the acceptance from our friends? Is that true happiness we feel when we do such and such activity, or is it just exciting? Do we really have wisdom, like everyone says, or are we just good at relaying popular ideas?

I don't intend to discuss each fruit or gift of the spirit and Satan's counterfeit. This topic is varied enough that it usually ends up being a rather personal, introspective endeavor. Because of this fact, it is usually a bad idea to go to your neighbor and say, "You are not happy! You are just experiencing Satan's counterfeit to happiness!" Apart from being terribly impolite, even if it were true, it would be unlikely to cause them to change their ways.

None of us are all that good at having the spirit with us absolutely all the time. This endeavor requires constant self-evaluation and adjustment. One good rule of

---

[4] D&C 20:77,79

thumb is that if we are being led to help and uplift others out of love, then that is a good sign.[5]

The fruits and gifts of the spirit are wonderful and vital to our spiritual progression, but they are not the focus, just like video games shouldn't be the focus of my children's chores. If my kids were to grow up and be successful adults by fulfilling all the tasks they undertake to the letter, but fulfill all those tasks with a mental timer that is constantly counting down to their next video game hour, I would have failed to raise my kids correctly. Life is more than just looking forward to our next video game fix, TV fix, or other frivolous activity. If we get too focused on the reward and not the lesson, we miss the point.[6]

What does this look like in spiritual matters? This happens when someone focuses so much on the emotional elation which come from the fruits and gifts of the spirit that they lose sight of the whole point of the spirit. In an effort to find ever increasing "spiritual highs," they begin seeking dramatic spiritual experiences or look for people who claim these experiences. They aren't as excited about the lessons or truths found in these experiences as they are in the dramatic emotions involved. You can often find people like this searching the internet for the most recent

---

[5] D&C 46:7-9
[6] Jacob 4:14

online spiritual movements: near death experiences, dramatic dreams or visions, detailed timelines on the second coming of Christ, or people claiming to have seen Christ face-to-face.

In the restored gospel of Jesus Christ, we claim to have many of these spiritual manifestations, so what's wrong with seeking after them? The difference lies in why we seek them. When we look for prophets, are we interested in what their message entails, or are we mainly interested in how the prophet got the message?

The online prophet is usually more than happy to share all the juicy details of every vision and each angel they've encountered with pages and pages of dramatic prose, while the message behind their purported visions is often extremely shallow or hopelessly muddled.

Spirituality isn't just about dramatic spiritual experiences. Our sole focus in life shouldn't be seeking after our next "spiritual high." Spirituality is not an online subscription to a class entitled, "How to See an Angel in Ten Easy Steps." Spirituality teaches us how to be angels in others' lives. We haven't achieved the epitome of spirituality when we receive a dramatic vision in which Jesus Christ visits us and we finally see his face. Our ultimate goal is for others to see his face through ours.[7]

---

[7] Moro. 7:46-48

We must be changed from selfish to selfless, from competitive to cooperative. This is the primary job of the Holy Ghost, to change us by cleansing and sanctifying us.[8] This process is sometimes called baptism of fire,[9] born of the spirit,[10] or commonly just born again.[11]

In the restored gospel of Jesus Christ, when we talk about baptism of fire, sometimes we just mean the ordinance of the Gift of the Holy Ghost. This ordinance is done directly after our baptism and entails authorized priesthood holders placing their hands on the head of the individual and saying, among other things, the words, "Receive the Holy Ghost."

While receiving the Holy Ghost is equivalent to baptism by fire, we are constantly instructed that this process is not complete when the hands are lifted from our head, but scarcely begun.[12]

In a similar way, the first few stages of heating metal ore in order to purify it are impressive and can seem to completely change everything in an instant, but it is just

---

[8] For a reference on cleansing, see Moro. 6:4. For references on sanctifying, see 3 Ne. 27:20 or 2 Thes. 2:13.
[9] See Matt. 3:11, 2 Ne. 31:13, or D&C 19:31
[10] See Moses 6:59-60
[11] see John 3:1-6. Note that this scripture describes born again as both baptism of water and spirit, not just baptism of fire.
[12] For a recent example of this type of instruction, see Bednar, David A. "Receive the Holy Ghost." General Conference, The Church of Jesus Christ of Latter-day Saints. Oct 2010.

the beginning. The later stages are many times hotter and can be much more complex.

Yes, at times you may feel like the Holy Ghost cleans and sanctifies you in an instant. In reality, the full process takes much longer. It takes longer than a lifetime to change us into someone like God. We talked about this in the previous section when we said repentance both cleansed us from sin and changed our natures through the atonement.[13]

So, which is it? Is it the Holy Ghost or Jesus Christ who cleanses us and sanctifies us? As we've seen so many times before, the answer is both. Christ implements the atonement in our lives, but the Holy Ghost must take an active part. This is because our hearts must be changed, and the Holy Ghost, as a personage of spirit, is the only one in the Godhead who can dwell in our hearts.[14]

Now we finally come to a full picture of the atonement. Christ's role is perhaps the most visible and most commonly discussed, but each other member of the Godhead also has a role in the atonement. In fact, you might say that having a role in the atonement is what makes someone a member of the Godhead.

---

[13] For references on cleansing, see Alma 5:27, 1 Jn. 1:7 or Morm. 9:6. For references on sanctifying, see D&C 20:31 or Heb. 13:12.
[14] D&C 130:22

Our Heavenly Parents created the Plan of Happiness along with the idea of the atonement in the first place. Jesus Christ volunteered to be the one to come down and be the foundation on which the implementation of the atonement rests. The Holy Ghost assented to be the primary medium through which the power of the atonement pours directly into our souls, purifying and sanctifying.

This may seem complicated, but in actuality, we see this same pattern all the time. We can successfully have an open-heart surgery thanks to the research doctors who developed the technique, the actual surgeon who performs your particular surgery, and the surgical implements and sterile environment. Without any of these three, the surgery fails.

In the business world, an idea is conceived, it is brought to fruition in a tangible product or process, and it is marketed to the consumers through reaching out in some form of advertising.

In the scientific world, the theorist comes up with a theory, the experimentalist tests and fleshes out the details of that theory, and the engineer takes the theory and finds an application to improve our lives.

The Godhead is unified in the effort of the atonement of all of us. They are naturally involved in all parts of the atonement, but one or the other has a more visible role in certain aspects. Pointing out that the Holy Ghost purifies us through the baptism of fire doesn't take anything away from Christ's role. Pointing out that Christ suffered for us in the Garden of Gethsemane and on the cross doesn't take anything away from our Heavenly Parents' role in actually devising and implementing the atonement. The Godhead is unified.[15] They work together without competition or pride.

Because of this, when initially reaching out to God in our lives, it doesn't matter which member of the Godhead we are most comfortable with. Any one will do. You may first reach out to Christ, as the example of compassion and love; the Holy Ghost, as the constant companion; or directly to God, as the benevolent father. The process of the atonement cleanses you from sin, completely changes who you are, and eventually restores you to life after death. This process can start with any member of the Godhead. It will not end there, however.

When you reach out to God on some level to begin your spiritual path, be prepared for a journey in which you do not dictate the details. Knowing God exists and beginning a relationship with him must be done on his terms, not ours.

---

[15] John 17:20-22

On this journey, we are often like my boys and their cleaning. We spend a whole lot of time intently walking through life while completely focused on all the exciting stuff life has to offer. Sometimes we carry a few spiritual or religious trinkets along to make it look convincing to ourselves and others, but we completely miss the focus. Becoming like God is the focus. That can only be done on his terms.

Conclusion

In this book, I have discussed the topics of God, Christ, and the Holy Ghost. My intent was to capture the essential basics and not get bogged down in the long process of filling in details or attempt to move beyond the basics. There is good reason for this. It is in reasoning out the details that you begin to fold the truths of the gospel into your life and get to know God personally.

If there existed a book that could perfectly describe God in every detail, large and small, reading it would still be insufficient. That would be like trying to tell my infant daughter that if I died tomorrow, she could just read my journals and watch all the family home videos to know who I was.

Yes, reading in order to know about God is important, but it will never replace getting to know God by building a relationship with him.

Joseph Smith made the same point when he said, "Could we read and comprehend all that has been written from the days of Adam, on the relation of man to God and angels in a future state, we should know very little about it. Reading the experience of others, or the revelation given to *them*, can never give *us* a comprehensive view of our condition and true relation to God. Knowledge of these things can only be obtained by experience through the ordinances of God set forth for that purpose. Could you gaze into heaven five minutes, you would know more than you would by reading all that ever was written on the subject."[1]

Of course, building a relationship with God doesn't mean we can ignore building a relationship with others or with organized religion. We must approach God, but we must do it on his terms. Our spiritual journey back to God must be our own, but we can't use that as license to traipse around wherever we feel like and ignore the path God is encouraging us to travel.

When my kids play with Lego bricks, if they completely ignore the instructions, they have fun but often can't get much beyond using a handful of pieces to make a few basic shapes. At the same time, if they only follow the instructions and never branch out, their attention only lasts until shortly after the instructions are finished. When they use the more advanced shapes and

---

[1] *Teachings of Presidents of the Church: Joseph Smith,* The Church of Jesus Christ of Latter-day Saints. 2007, pg. 419.

concepts found in the instructions to make personal variations or build their own creations, that is when they truly get the concept.

This book has never been intended as a complete picture of the restored gospel of Jesus Christ but a launching point for the Latter-day Saint's spiritual journey. We have been taught the basics over and over in primary class and Sunday school, but sometimes we see them as separate pieces and never quite get around to connecting them into much more than a couple basic shapes. Other times we treat the rules and standards as nothing more than a list of instructions to complete, without ever gaining a deeper understanding of the gospel of Jesus Christ and without allowing the truths of the gospel to feed our soul.

The restored gospel, from the very beginning, has always come with a note saying, "Some assembly required." It is in our fumbling to make things fit into our lives and in our tripping steps back to God that we learn to trust in him. When we trust in God, we naturally begin to build a relationship with him. That relationship is the primary manner we accomplish the true aim of this life—to one day become like him.

Made in United States
Troutdale, OR
11/30/2023